SC
FOR

The Traveler's Guide to Make The Most Out of Your Trip to Scotland - *Where to Go, Eat,* Sleep & Party

By Dagny Taggart

© Copyright 2015

All rights reserved. No portion of this book may be reproduced -mechanically, electronically, or by any other means, including photocopying- without the permission of the publisher. Some of the images may belong to Stephen Bailey, who has agreed completely to allow their distribution on this guide.

Disclaimer

The information provided in this book is designed to provide helpful information on the subjects discussed. The author's books are only meant to provide the reader with the basics travel guidelines of a certain location, without any warranties regarding the accuracy of the information and advice provided. Each traveler should do their own research before departing

Table of Contents

My FREE Gift to You! 8

Learn Any Language 300% FASTER 9

Introduction: Are You Ready for an Amazing Journey? 10

Chapter 1: Welcome to Scotland! 12

    Scotland at a glance 12
    Iconic Experiences...13
    Unique Experiences 15
    How to Use This Guide..16

Chapter 2: Let's Start At the Beginning - Planning Your Trip..........18

    When To Go and Understanding Different Seasons 18
    Travel Costs and Organizing Your Money 19
    Example Budgets for a Scotland Trip 19
    Example Costs in Scotland 20
        Easy Ways to Reduce Your Costs When Traveling in Scotland..........21
        Organizing Your Money 22

    Basic Travel Requirements...23
    Getting to Scotland 24
    Getting Around and Planning Your Transport..............................24
        Suburban City Transport 25
        Nationwide Train Network..25
        Scotland's Bus Network..25
        Hiring a Car 25
        Internal Flights 26

    Ferry Services 26
    Where to Stay 26

Chapter 3: Immersing Yourself in Scotland (Culture, Accent, Manners) 29

Scotland, Britain, and the UK 29
Scottish Pride 29
Understanding Traditions and Contemporary Scottish Culture 30
Understanding the Scottish Accent 31
Scottish Tourist Information 31
Recommendations from your Accommodation 32
Staying Safe *32*
Staying Healthy *32*

Chapter 4: About the Upcoming Destination Chapters 34

Chapter 5: Edinburgh 36

Travel Essentials for Edinburgh 36
Edinburgh Experiences 37
Edinburgh In Two Days 38
Old Town *38*
New Town *40*

Edinburgh in Four Days or More 41
Historic Attractions 41
Exploring the City 42
Galleries and Gardens 42
More to Discover in Edinburgh 43
Edinburgh's August Festivals 43
The Best Places to Eat and Drink in Edinburgh 44

Chapter 6: Glasgow 46

Travel Essentials for Glasgow 46
Glasgow Experiences 48

In One Day 48
With Three Days or More 50
Art and Museums 50
In the Evenings 51

Places to Relax and Explore 52
Something Different 53

Where to Eat and Drink in Glasgow 53

Chapter 7: The Central Belt 55

Travel Essentials for the Central Belt 55
Central Belt Experiences 56
Itinerary Planning 56
Stirlingshire (accessed from Glasgow and Edinburgh) 56
Lothian (Accessed from Edinburgh) 58
Clydeside (accessed from Glasgow) 59

Chapter 8: Southern Scotland 61

Travel Essentials for Southern Scotland 61
Southern Scotland Experiences 62
The Scottish Borders 62
Southwest Scotland 64

Chapter 9: North East Scotland 67

Travel Essentials for North East Scotland 68
North East Scotland Experiences 69
In a Few Days 69

In a Week or More 72

Chapter 10: The Scottish Highlands and Islands 76

Travel Essentials for the Scottish Highlands 77
Scottish Highlands Experiences 78
   Less than One Week 78
   With a Week or More 82

Chapter 12: Thanks for Reading! 86

Learn Any Language 300% FASTER 87

   PS: CAN I ASK YOU A QUICK FAVOR? 88

Preview Of "Italy For Tourists - The Traveler's Travel Guide to Make the Most Out of Your Trip to Italy - Where to Go, Eat, Sleep & Party" 89

Check Out My Other Books 100

About the Author 101

Dedicated to those who love going beyond their own frontiers.

Keep on traveling,

Dagny Taggart

My FREE Gift to You!

As a way of saying thank you for downloading my book, I'd like to send you an exclusive gift that will revolutionize the way you learn new languages. It's an extremely comprehensive PDF with 15 language hacking rules that **will help you learn 300% faster, with less effort, and with higher than ever retention rates**.

This guide is an amazing complement to the book you just got, and could easily be a stand-alone product, but for now I've decided to give it away for free, to thank you for being such an awesome reader, and to make sure I give you all the value that I can to help you succeed faster on your language learning journey.

To get your FREE gift, go to the link below, follow the steps, and I'll send it to your email address right away.

>> http://bitly.com/Language-Gift <<

Learn Any Language 300% FASTER

>> Get Full Online Language Courses With Audio Lessons <<

Would you like to learn a new language before you start your trip? I think that's a great idea. Now, why don't you do it 300% *FASTER*?

I've partnered with the most revolutionary language teachers to bring you the very language online courses I've ever seen. It's a mind-blowing program specifically created for language hackers such as ourselves. It will allow you learn ANY language, from French to Chinese, 3x faster, straight from the comfort of your own home, office, or wherever you may be. It's like having an unfair advantage!

You can choose from a wide variety of languages, such as French, Spanish, Italian, German, Chinese, Portuguese, and A TON more.

Each Online Course consists of:

+ 91 Built-In Lessons
+ 33 Interactive Audio Lessons
+ 24/7 Support to Keep You Going

The program is extremely engaging, fun, and easy-going. You won't even notice you are learning a complex foreign language from scratch. And before you realize it, by the time you go through all the lessons you will officially become a truly solid speaker.

Old classrooms are a thing of the past. It's time for a revolution.

If you'd like to go the extra mile, follow the link below, and let the revolution begin!

>> http://www.bitly.com/foreign-language-courses <<

CHECK OUT THE COURSE »

Introduction
Are You Ready for an Amazing Journey?

Scotland revels in its authenticity. As Europe moves closer towards a monotone culture and travel experience, this rugged northern nation showcases something entirely original. Landscapes roll uninhabited and untrammeled, deserted beaches hide beneath cliffs, tiny villages evoke impressions of yesteryear, and there's no limit to the adventure. Scotland is nothing like England. It's also hard to compare with the rest of Europe. Here's a country that genuinely delights in welcoming visitors, and one that offers irrefutable opportunities for exploration.

Rugged and dramatic, Scotland's land is almost unparalleled, rolling green across the country and cascading onto hidden beaches. It's rural and unchanged for centuries, winding roads passing dry stone walls and villages seemingly screaming of antiquity. Cities provide a new angle, Edinburgh and Glasgow vastly different but equally compelling. Throughout it all there's never any denying where you are. While the referendum for independence saw Scotland stay as part of the Great Britain, the country remains as unique as ever.

For many visitors, Scotland is seen as an addition to visiting London and England. Then they arrive and wonder why Scotland wasn't the prime consideration on the itinerary. Its reputation sometimes precedes itself. If English weather is considered bad, then Scotland's is terrible. If England's food is fried, then Scotland's comes with an extra three inches of fat. This is the country that batters and deep fries Mars Bars after all. Yet there's charming impressions to be gleamed from preconceptions and stereotypes; like the man in a kilt playing bagpipes, sessions drinking the world's finest whisky, and wild camping in fields of heather.

Scotland always leaves indelible memories. It offers bags of charm and some of the world's most pristine landscapes. Then there's the castles and historic ruins. And it's appeal stretches across audiences, despite that outside the famous city of Edinburgh, it's a country that's generally reserved for the more intrepid of visitors. Anyone with a fondness for being outdoors tends to walk into a wonderland, the wilderness a mecca for hiking and off the beaten track journeys. Those keen on culture find genuine local encounters that are increasingly difficult to experience in Europe. And anyone with a sense of adventure discovers a country that's handcrafted for every visitor.

So jump forward into a country that responds to the cute cliches; yes you will see kilts, hear some bagpipes, and sip whisky with a view of a mountain loch. But you'll also experience a country that reserves its best for those that visit.

Chapter 1:
Welcome to Scotland!

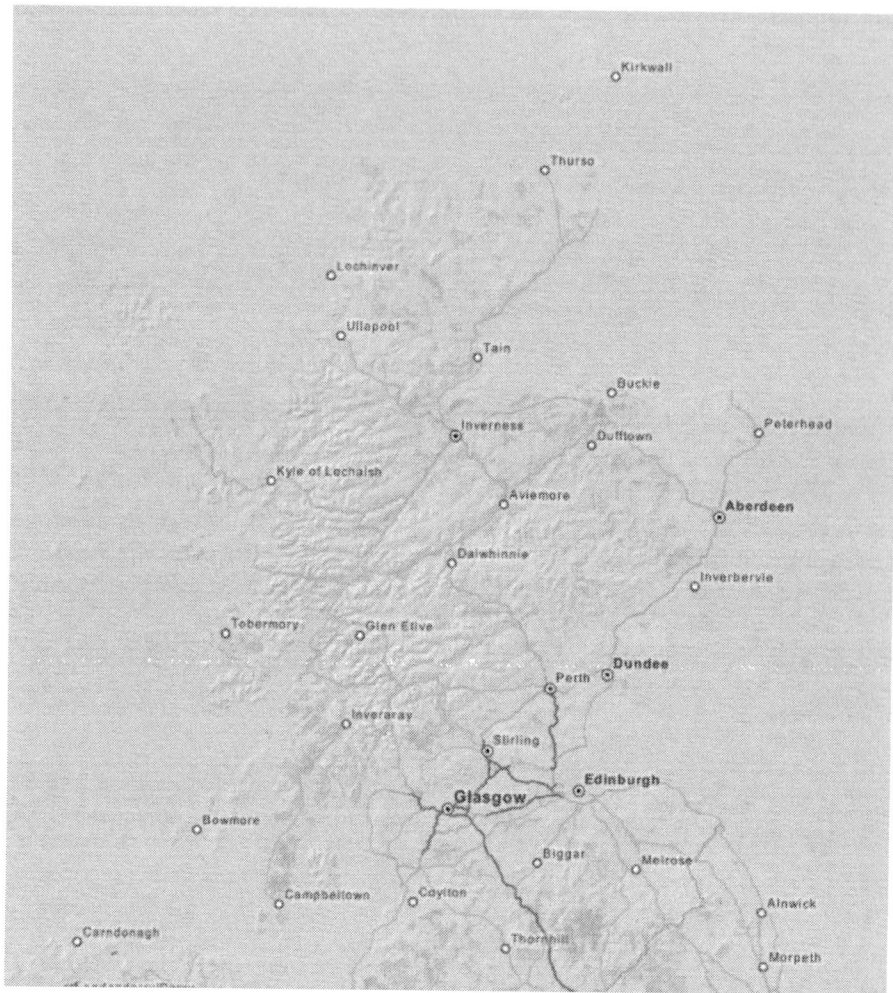

Scotland at a glance

Scotland is a relatively small country that bristles with history. Tucked away in the North Sea, it neighbors England to the south and forms part of the United Kingdom of Great Britain. It's a sparsely populated country, the majority of Scots living in a narrow band of urban development running east to west across the country. This is where you'll find the two major cities of Glasgow and Edinburgh. Further north, the geography becomes precipitous and theatrical, never a mile of flat land as the mountains rise and the valleys role. This rural part of Scotland is dotted with villages and cute towns, most of them reminiscent of a bygone era and a launching point for outdoor adventure.

Edinburgh is the most famous drawcard, the capital city laced with history and rarely disappointing. Nearby Glasgow often gets a rough ride through vast ranging stereotypes. While Edinburgh has the architecture, Glasgow offers hipness and vibrant culture that's iconically Scottish. These cities are merely an hour apart and both are the main transport hubs. The country's two major international airports are found in Edinburgh and Glasgow and they're also the terminus for the high speed train lines from London and England.

These cities (usually Edinburgh) provide the most common starting point for a Scotland trip. Those with just a few days tend to stick to the cities with the potential for a day trip into the wilderness. Anyone with longer has an open book regarding potential itineraries. Scotland is small, and while the roads are winding and sometimes slow, the country's infrastructure enables visitors to see a lot in a limited amount of time.

Throughout it all there's an atmosphere of openness and humor. Scots are fiercely proud of being Scottish and this is often manifested as defining their difference from England. It's generally quieter, more relaxed, and more welcoming. However, it's not always traditional notions of welcome. They make jokes, nod heads, and may not even smile. The red carpet isn't laid out for foreign visitors. Few receive special treatment. Yet immerse yourself in the local style and the Scots are quick to open up and integrate you into their ways.

The country's tourist infrastructure is good, although the rurality means that you can sometimes be on your own in the middle of nowhere. Which is often Scotland's appeal. Come here to get lost. Come here to explore. Come here to soak up a unique culture and most importantly, come to to a country that delights in its authenticity.

Iconic Experiences

- **Edinburgh's** castle and ancient architecture has been inspiring visitors for centuries. The capital city is the country's number one destination, home to comedy festivals, trumpet blowing guards, streets of cobblestone, and much more. (Chapter 5).

- **Glasgow** runs on a different rhythm. It's a city of the alternative and underground, continual surprises hiding behind the working class facade. Undeniably fun and irrevocably original, Glasgow is a city that rewards everyone who gives it a chance. (Chapter 6).

- Great day trips can be enjoyed around the Central Belt, the finest being the historic town of **Stirling** with its castle, battlefields, and distillery. (Chapter 7).

- **Southern Scotland** is a region of rolling valleys, dramatic **castle ruins**, and beautiful abbeys in minuscule villages. (Chapter 8).

- **St. Andrews and Perth** are two of Europe's finest coastal towns, radiating history and commanding beautifully green locations along the eastern seashore. (Chapter 9).

- Britain's highest mountain epitomizes the rugged adventure of Scotland and the astonishing scenery of the Scottish Highlands. **Ben Nevis** is a challenging day climb, taking you above an uninhabited landscape of lochs and one of Europe's final stretches of wilderness. (Chapter 10).

Scottish Highland scenery

Unique Experiences

- It may not be the Alps, but Scotland's ski slopes make for great winter entertainment. They're located in the heart of nowhere in the Cairngorms National park, the action on the slopes combined with tiny tiny villages with as many pubs as houses. (Chapters 9 and 10).

- Windswept, remote, and practically unchanged for millennia, the western Highland coastline is one of the strangest beach destinations on the planet. When the sun shines the beaches are easily amongst the best in Europe, and when it rains, the cliffs have enough wild charm to keep you company. (Chapter 10).

- Climb to two millennia old Arthur's Seat for glorious vistas onto the historic center of Edinburgh. (Chapter 5).

Arthur's Seat and the view over Edinburgh

- Glasgow Cathedral and Tenement House prove that Scotland's iconic architecture isn't just found in the capital. (Chapter 6).

- Rosslyn Chapel was made famous by *The Da Vinchi Code* and it looks every bit a fictional creation. (Chapter 7).

- Seaside Dunbar is a charming base for a few days as you tuck into fish and chips and leisurely hiking trails. (Chapter 8).

- Scotland is to whisky what France is to champagne and Italy is to pizza. Dozens of distilleries can be found across the country, most of them revealing centuries of history and opening their doors for **whisky tasting**. Even those that don't like whisky come away with new found adoration. South East Scotland is the heart of the country's whisky culture. (Chapter 9).

How to Use This Guide

This guidebook is split into distinct sections that lead you through the best that Scotland has to offer. It includes all the essential information to make your visit a reality. This guidebook covers the whole of the country, from the enchantment of Edinburgh to hiking trails on a remote field of wandering sheep. Scotland is a relatively easy country to travel in. English is the local language (albeit with a sometimes indecipherable accent) and there's a well defined tourist infrastructure. Accommodation is usually cute although rarely luxurious, and getting involved with tradition comes from the moment you land.

What this guidebook doesn't do is provide reams of listings detailing the average and mundane. If it's good then this guidebook tells you about it. If it's not so good, then why waste time reading about it. The country is also too laid-back and untouched to arrive with an exacting plan. Really experiencing Scotland requires an openness that the country is quick to imbue. This guidebook aims to provide everything to get you started and immersed. Scotland will invariably do the rest. But that's not to say that it's sparse on content. This guidebook is both planning tool, immersive partner, and Scotland travel companion.

Chapter 2 is dedicated to planning your Scotland trip. It includes detailed information on how to get there, how to get around, planning an itinerary, and where to sleep. There's a section on costs and how to limit them, as well as indicative pricing to plan a budget. Scotland is unique and chapter 3 is all about ensuring you're prepared for the culture and customs of the country.

Kilts, bagpipes, whisky? Chapter 3 deconstructs the myths and ensures you're ready for what the country is actually like. Experiencing traditions is a major highlight of Scotland so it's good to learn a little about what you'll be eating, the slang for saying hello, and what to order in a two centuries old pub.

A whisky distillery in Eastern Scotland.

Chapters 4 - 10 contain the detailed information on Scotland's destinations. They're arranged geographically and spider web out from Edinburgh and Glasgow. Each chapter links to the next but is also self-contained. There's an introduction with entry points, transport, travel practicalities, and links to other geographical regions. Then the detail takes you on a journey across the region.

Chapter 2:
Let's Start At the Beginning - Planning Your Trip

When To Go and Understanding Different Seasons

Scotland's weather is the sole reason for the country's relative lack of visitors. Few places in the world are as beautiful yet see such limited numbers of tourists. Gaze across and the landscape offer an often mythical view. But look up and there's a good chance of seeing a gray sky. Scotland is unquestionably wet, often cold, and rarely sunny. In a way the weather is part of the appeal; there's a mystery to the low-hanging mist and a deeper feeling of being alone with nature when your feet are going numb. However, Scotland on a clear day is transformed. When the blue sky reflects off the alpine lochs there are few more splendid countries on the planet.

Trying to plan a trip based on the weather is challenging. It's anybody's guess when the sun will shine, so fastidiously analyzing the weather charts often leads to frustration. You may pick the two supposed driest weeks. Then it rains and you get annoyed. It's better to plan for all eventualities, brace yourself for poor weather, and then get delighted when the sun does shine. In general prices go up during the British school summer holiday period of mid-July to end-August. Along with Christmas and New Year, this is peak season. Almost every time outside these months is low season.

It's not all bad in Scotland. While it's not a tropical island, the weather shouldn't be off-putting. Here's what to expect.

Summer (June to August) – Peak travel season and the warmest months of the year. Edinburgh can get very busy in July and August (especially during the festival season) but the rest of the country doesn't feature the mass tourist overcrowding as elsewhere in Europe. Summer means long hours of daylight, making it a great time to be outdoors.

Autumn (September to November) – As the days shorten, Scotland shepherds in unpredictable weather. Often windy but occasionally fine, autumn is a good time for seeing a lot of the country. In October the clocks change which usually confirms the end of longer summer days and the start of short winter daylight hours.

Winter – (December – February) – Scotland in winter can be magical. With fields of snow glistening and mountains peeking above the mist, there's usually a visual enticement to counteract the cold. The country can also be drab and dreary with the long hours of darkness off-putting. It's generally too cold to be outside so most people stick to the cities and ski fields.

Spring (March to May) – While still unpredictable, spring is usually the driest time in Scotland. As the days lengthen and the greenery returns, this is also perhaps the most beautiful time of year. Quiet in terms of visitor numbers outside Easter.

Fall colors on the Isle of Skye

Travel Costs and Organizing Your Money

By European standards, Scotland is a relatively cheap country to travel in. It's a good 30% cheaper than England and outside Edinburgh, most find that their pounds can go a long way. Transport is generally cheap, budget accommodation is extremely good value, and much of Scotland is available for free, including the national parks. Scotland can cater for a range of budgets and for a range of vacation styles.

Example Budgets for a Scotland Trip

The Scots are the first to kick up a fuss when prices rise to overinflated levels. They're predominantly a working class bunch and they don't like getting ripped off. This attitude seems to filter through the tourism industry. Value is a mainstay of the experience and that helps keep costs down.

Estimating a budget for a Scotland trip heavily depends on the amount of time spent in Edinburgh. The city's prices dwarf those of the rest of the country, although they're nowhere near what's found in London, south of the border. The following provides a rough guide of what to expect in the majority of Scotland – add on 30% for spending most or all of your time in Edinburgh. All prices in British pounds.

- **Budget traveler (£30 - 45)** – This mainly constitutes cooking your own meals, often camping, and choosing the cheapest form of transport. Certainly achievable. In fact, with a lot of time spent in national parks and trip can even be cheaper than this.

- **Conscientious traveler (£40 – 60)** – A decent sized budget that's good enough to take in the best that Scotland has to offer. That means good value accommodation, traveling to remote areas, cooking some meals, but having money left over to eat and drink out.

- **Standard traveler - (£60 – 100)** – This budget should be enough for everything Scotland has to offer, outside the luxury end retreats. The hardest part of sticking within budget is not succumbing to a £200+ bottle of whisky at one of the distilleries.

- **Upmarket traveler (£100 - 200)** – Spend more and the country's fine dining restaurants and opulent retreats can also feature in the itinerary.

- **Luxury traveler (£200 +)** - Scotland has a number of luxurious and expensive resorts that deliver on a promise of solitude and untamed surroundings. It's these that are made available with a luxury budget.

Example Costs in Scotland

To give you a better idea of the costs, here are some mid-range travel essentials to be found in Scotland.

- A place to pitch a tent – Free - £8pp

- A dorm bed - £10 – 15pp

- A double in a dorm or budget hotel - £30 - 60

- A pint of beer - £3.00 – £3.50

- Traditional meal for two with drinks at a good but not gourmet restaurant - £25

- Journey of 200 miles by public transport - £10

- Full day guided tour of famous natural attraction – ranges from £20 – 80

- National park entrance - Free

- Takeaway lunch with coffee from a cafe - £5 - 7

Easy Ways to Reduce Your Costs When Traveling in Scotland

Scotland's costs can be further reduced with a few easy tricks. This might not mean your overall budget is reduced, more that more time and money is spent hanging out with the locals in one of the thousands of traditional pubs.

- **Book long distance trains and buses in advance** – There's a confusing long distance public transport pricing system in Scotland, with ticket prices dependent when you travel, when you book, and whatever the computer decides to spew out. For example, an Edinburgh to London train could cost £20. It could cost £300. Booking in advance for long distance travel is a huge money saver, especially for rail travel.

- **Travel outside peak hours** – Long distance travel is also much cheaper outside peak hours. These are Monday to Friday, before 09:30 and 15:30 – 18:00.

- **Avoid July and August** – Scotland only has a short peak season, from mid-July to the end of August. It's when the kids are off school and the prices are inflated. Anytime outside these months is cheaper.

- **Don't limit yourself to Edinburgh** – While the capital is the country's premier drawcard, Scotland has far to offer than a castle and some old buildings. Much like visitors to England, many hardly ever make it out of the capital. Leave Edinburgh and not only will you see more, it will be cheaper.

- **Take advantage of local midweek offers** – Many establishments entice the crowds by offering cut price deals during the week. In particular, pubs and restaurants will offer two for one dinners and half price drinks to bring in the punters. It makes for exceptional value.

Organizing Your Money

Scotland should pose no problems for accessing your money. Visa and mastercard are readily accepted and ATMs can be found in every town and city. As you head further north, the towns become further and further apart, so carrying a stash of cash is always advisable. Currency exchange is available in banks on the high street with most major currencies accepted. Note that this is often tailored towards Scots traveling abroad, so look around for the best rates.

Scotland and England both use the same pound, the one featuring the head of Queen Elizabeth II. It's a relatively stable currency that's generally worth $1.50 - $1.70. However, Scottish and English banknotes are different, despite being the same currency. In Scotland, both are accepted and interchangeable. If you plan to travel to England then watch out: Scottish banknotes are generally not accepted. You'll need to visit a bank to get them changed.

Eilean Donan Castle

Basic Travel Requirements

The interchangeable use of Scotland, Britain, and UK, often leads to confusion. Here's the basics. Scotland is one of the states that form the United Kingdom of Great Britain, a country governed ultimately by Queen Elizabeth II. The other members are England, Wales, and Northern Ireland. The UK, or Britain, has a single immigration office. Enter any of these countries and you'll be stamped into the UK. Travel between these countries and you won't be required to show a passport. However, if you're on a short term visa, remember that visiting Scotland and returning to England won't mean getting a new visa or extended stay.

US, Canadian, and Australian, visitors do not need a visa to enter the UK as a tourist. UK immigration officials can be touchy and will usually require proof that you've come on vacation. Most importantly, that means evidence of a return flight or onward ticket. Printing off hotel reservations and an itinerary is also helpful. In some cases, you may be required to prove that you have sufficient funds for the duration of your trip.

Other nationalities can check the UK entry requirements at www.gov.uk/check-uk-visa.

Despite being part of the European Union, the UK is not part of the European Schengen visa agreement. A Schengen visa valid for borderless travel in Europe will not be valid in the UK.

Getting to Scotland

Getting to Scotland is relatively straightforward, regardless of where you're traveling from. There are many options for arriving directly. Other visitors may prefer to use the opportunity to combine England and Scotland into one trip.

By Air: Edinburgh and Glasgow are the two main international airports. While they only have limited intercontinental flights, there are dozens of daily connections to London. Therefore most long-distance flight itineraries will land in Scotland via London Heathrow or Gatwick. Both airports, along with Aberdeen and Inverness, have numerous direct connections to Western and Eastern Europe. Budget airlines Easyjet and Ryanair offer some excellent bargains when flying form other European cities.

By Land: Arriving by land means coming from England. The most comfortable and quickest is the two high speed train lines that run from London to Edinburgh / Glasgow and then onwards to Inverness in the Scottish Highlands. One route travels along England's East Coast, the other along the West. Both connect in Edinburgh and Glasgow. London to Edinburgh takes between four and five hours. It's far slower by bus and not recommended if you're traveling from the south of England. Even from cities like Newcastle and Manchester, it's more enjoyable and double the speed by train.

By Boat: Scheduled ferry services connect Scotland to the Netherlands, Scandinavia, and Ireland.

Getting Around and Planning Your Transport

Scotland is a rural country. Other than a thin strip of cities and development, the experience is very much marked by rolling mountains and roads that curve and then curve some more. Getting around is never particularly fast and some forward planning is required. There might only be one bus service to your destination a day and some train services will only stop on request. However, getting around shouldn't be overly challenging. Everybody speaks English and is invariably keen to help.

Suburban City Transport

Most destinations in Scotland are small enough to preclude requiring suburban transport. Edinburgh and Glasgow are the exceptions and there are good local bus networks to use. The locals love to complaint that the bus is late / expensive / not what it used to be / slow. But that merely reflects their delight at poking fun at the establishment. You should find the services more than adequate.

Nationwide Train Network

High speed rail lines continue past Edinburgh to Inverness and Northern Scotland. These are fast and affordable and cut through beautiful swathes of Scottish hinterland. Slower local trains head out to many corners of the country. One line runs along the west coast from Glasgow to Fort William, another connects Edinburgh to Dundee, then Aberdeen and Inverness on the East Coast. Trains also run north from Inverness to the very tip of the country. Scotland's size means that trains are a pleasant way of traveling. Even if they go slow, it's not that far between destinations.

Scotland's Bus Network

Winding to all corners, Scotland's bus network has been taking pensioners to village markets for decades. Outside the central urban belt, the network can often feel like a stereotype; buses that only run a couple of times a day, bus stops overgrown by bushes, routes that detour for no apparent reason. Some will find it slow, others may find it necessary. The buses are cheaper than the trains although they're not as comfortable. To reach rural areas, any major town or city is a good starting point.

Hiring a Car

For many visitors, hiring a car is the easiest way of getting around the country. It's especially recommended for visiting the Scottish Highlands and North East Scotland, as public transport is inconsistent and might not exist at all in some places. International and local car hire firms have been competing over prices for the last 20 years, gradually driving them down until a cheap car can be found for less than £30 a day. High petrol prices are softened by short distances, and in rural Scotland, parking is never hard to come by. Driving is generally easy, even if it's done on the left hand side of the road.

The exception is winter, when hazardous ice can be problematic, especially after dark. In rural Scotland, there are few other drivers on the road. However, in the urban belt around Glasgow and Edinburgh driving can be chaotic. Rather than hire a car at the airport, a good option is to hire a car after you've explored Glasgow and Edinburgh.

Internal Flights

Scotland isn't really big enough to make internal flights a sensible option. It's been included here due to the variety of flights available from Scotland to England. Small Scottish airports aren't limited to planes flying south to London. There are cheap flights to Manchester, Liverpool, Cornwall, and more. These are very useful for anyone on a longer England and Scotland vacation. Especially useful is Inverness as a gateway to the Highlands.

Ferry Services

Scotland's outlying islands are serviced by trundling war horses of public ferries (sometimes with an iconic long grey bearded skipper, most of the time not). If you're heading out to the islands then details on the ferries are found in chapter 10.

Where to Stay

Scotland's accommodation is invariably Scottish. Without even trying, it responds to the preconceptions people have when dreaming about a Scottish vacation. Guesthouses are often owner-managed by cute old couples with thick accents, the breakfasts come with dollops of black pudding, and the furniture is often boutique without realizing. There would be something missing if it was anything different. Experiencing Scotland is elevated by its accommodation, from cute farmhouse cottages to hostels on the edge of a mountain range. It's also exceptional value and cheaper than what's found in England.

For decades, centuries perhaps, Scottish accommodation was focused on the local inn. This was often a few tatty bedrooms above the local pub in town, with a pint of mild offered on arrival and a 12 item fried breakfast in the morning. Such places still exist, although Scotland's tourism industry has become far more sophisticated since them; fear not fried bacon lovers, the huge breakfasts remain a mainstay.

The general style is to be low-key and intimate. Many major hotel chains are represented in the cities, but across rural Scotland, the accommodation is usually 100% Scottish. And what the guesthouses lack in modern touches, they more than make for with coatings of tradition. Individual destinations add local touches; bars selling whisky from the nearby distillery, endless vistas, or blankets in the local tartan.

Throughout Scotland, booking in advance is recommended. For Edinburgh and Glasgow it means cheaper prices as many hotels offer deals on sites like www.booking.com. In rural Scotland, a quick phone call ensures there's somebody at reception when you arrive and the bar has been adequately stocked. There's often no need to book far in advance. Travel plans can remain flexible with morning phone calls made to reserve the next guesthouse. Accommodation owners are unquestionably the best source of information about accommodation in your next destination and they'll often do the reserving for you.

Traditional star ratings are not always applicable so don't fret if a place doesn't have one. VisitScotland, the country's tourism board, has a localized graded quality assurance scheme. VisitScotland also has a comprehensive list of all accommodation registered with them. Coming under the VisitScotland banner requires certain standards and markers of quality. Their website has an excellent search facility - www.visitscotland.com/accommodation/

Campsites, Caravans, and Holiday Parks (£5 - £15pp) - Camping in the wilds of Scotland is an iconic experience, the tent battered by wind and rocking in a field of purple heather. Free wild camping is in the process of being banned but there are dozens of campsites that fulfill the idyllic image of camping in Scotland. For something a little more comfortable, you'll find campsites and caravan parks across the country. Expect clean ablution facilities, electricity hookups, and static caravans available to hire.

Hostels (£10 – £20pp) – Scotland's hostels really evoke traditional notions of a hostel. No, not a cramped dorm in a European capital with couples getting on in the dorm above your head. More like a youth hostel in a rural area; a place where hikers and an eclectic mix of ages convene. While they're usually simple, Scottish hostels often occupy wonderful positions and are excellent choices for hiking and exploring the outdoors.

Bed and Breakfasts and Guesthouses (£20 – £200pp) – The core of Scotland's accommodation is the huge network of B&Bs and guesthouses. The majority are owner-managed which ensures excellent service and quality. In general, you get what you pay for. Cheaper options will be clean and basic. Four and five star options may come with jacuzzis overlooking the highlands or regal interiors. Most noticeable in this category is the distinctiveness of the accommodation. Each will be memorable because each is different.

Hotels (£40 – £200pp) – Generally more luxurious and more expensive than guesthouses, although the boundary between hotel and guesthouse is increasingly blurred. They tend to offer more staff, more rooms, and not necessarily better quality for the price. A more usable option in the cities.

Self-catering (£15 – 100pp) – An increasingly popular choice are self-catering cottages, units, and apartments. These are often rented out for a minimum of three nights. Found throughout the country, they're widely used as a base by groups, families, and couples. Like the guesthouses, quality varies and you get what you pay for.

Something different (£100pp +) - Scotland revels in its authenticity and when it comes to splurging there's always something memorable to find. Like converted castles, boutique cottages in the forest, or wooden houses overlooking serene lakes. The VisitScotland website has many ideas for a special night or two.

Chapter 3:
Immersing Yourself in Scotland (Culture, Accent, Manners)

Scotland is a unique country and getting the most from it requires a certain understanding of the local psyche. The country is nothing like England (and making comparisons of the sort can be perceived as rude). It's a place where traditions live on and a fierce local pride is omnipresent. This chapter provides the background information that enables you to easily slip into the local rhythm. It covers where you are, how to think locally, how to understand the accent, and how to get the most from the country.

Scotland, Britain, and the UK

First, a quick handle on the country you're visiting. Officially, Scotland is part of the UK (along with England, Wales, and Ireland) and a 2014 referendum saw the Scots narrowly vote in favor of staying this way. However, cynics will argue that the independence movement only failed because of a lack of charismatic local leaders. Scotland has its own parliament and locally organizes many services within the country – including the excellent tourist information service. However, it remains a part of the United Kingdom.

Scottish Pride

Despite voting against independence, the Scots are as proud a nation as anywhere in Europe. They're stoically Scottish, something that usually comes with heavy hints of self-degradation. The Scots may regularly complain about Scotland but don't be caught doing the same; they're not sympathetic to anyone criticizing the homeland. This pride in being Scottish provides an authenticity and intimacy to traveling in the country. Everything is evocatively Scottish and being immersed in it starts from the moment you set foot in the country.

Castle Stalker

Understanding Traditions and Contemporary Scottish Culture

Haggis, tartan kilts, bagpipes? Travel reverie about Scotland comes with many classic images. Here's the good part. These traditions are very much part of modern Scotland, even though the Loch Ness Monster still hasn't been found. It's almost impossible to travel here and not be tempted to lift up a kilt and see if it's true about not wearing underwear. The traditions of Scotland are what continue to excite travelers and there's no let up; whisky tasting, archaic local pubs, strange local foods, ginger beards, eating breakfast fried in several inches of oil. While some may argue that Scotland is behind the times economically (which could be true), there's a wonderful continuation of tradition that forms the basis of contemporary Scottish culture.

In the most part, this is a working class country. Saying hello and sharing a greeting is part of culture and the Scots will be quick to let you in. However, this isn't where you'll find waitresses fussing over your order, ubiquitous smiles, and a culture of the customer is always right. The Scots are welcoming in their own peculiar way and sometimes it takes a while to see a smile. As a tourist, you won't receive any preferential treatment. And this should be seen as a positive. It ensures that you really feel part of the country you've exploring.

Understanding the Scottish Accent

Scotland holds a place in the highest echelons of indecipherable accents. They speak fast, use oodles of slang, and shorten many words. All of which makes it confusing, especially if English isn't your first language. Historically, the Scottish accent came as a blend of local language and English in the 17th century.

Here are a few of the most common examples:
- Ah – I
- Aye – yes
- Baltic – very cold
- Ben – down
- Blootered – very drunk
- Cannae – can not
- How no'? - why not?
- Isnae – is not
- Ken – know
- Lassie – female
- Radge – crazy
- Yin – one (referring to a person or object, not a number)

Don't be afraid to ask someone to speak slower so you can understand. They won't be offended. In fact, they might be proud to discover that their accent really is very Scottish. Furthermore, many Scots use a continuum of accents to define their speak. In formal situations they'll use less slang than with family and friends. In most situations they switch to their formal language to help foreigners understand. To get a real picture on the variety of Scottish accents, try reading an Irvine Welsh book. He's the author of *Trainspotting* and his first person characters range from barely Scottish to impossible to read.

Scottish Tourist Information

Continuing the theme of Scottish pride, VisitScotland do a wonderful job in promoting the inimitable and exceptional to be found in the country. This is the country's national tourism organization and their website is an extremely good resource, especially when traveling to remote parts of the country. Unfortunately, budget cuts have meant a reduction in the number of dedicated tourist information offices around the country, making the

VisitScotland website and even more integral tool (www.visitscotland.com). In particular, there's a very good accommodation search facility.

National park visitors centers are also useful for detailed information on hiking trails and routes through the parks. They usually have free information on other national parks in the country.

Recommendations from your Accommodation

Arguably the finest source of local information is the person that checks you into your accommodation. They'll know which pub is doing two for one dinners on a Tuesday, what hiking trail is most suitable to a couple in their fifties, and exactly what's available in the local area. As most accommodation is owner-managed, expect detailed information that's been gleamed over the last 30 years. Most accommodation features an area where local businesses leave their flyers and information and you may also find reams of information in your hotel room.

Staying Safe

Scotland is a relatively safe country to visit. Crime against tourists is limited and it's rare that visitors encounter any problems. Any crime against tourists is usually opportunistic rather than planned. The usual precautions apply. The exception might be the rowdy weekend scenes to be found in city centers after midnight, a congregation of drunk people sometimes determined to create havoc. It's unlikely that you'll see this and the problem is not city wide. It's usually restricted to one downtrodden part of a city center.

A more relevant challenge can be the Scottish wilderness. When the rain beats down and the wind thunders across the valleys, being outside isn't always pleasant. Even when you set off hiking on a sunny day, it's essential to come prepared for all potential eventualities. Underestimating how cold it can get in the Scottish Highlands can make for frozen toes. Likewise, going for a midnight dip in the lake after a few whiskies has given many a tourist hypothermia.

Staying Healthy

When the whiffs of fried mars bars float down a high street, you would be forgiven for thinking that Scotland is an unhealthy nation. Sure, the local diet may mean an increase in waist size, but Scotland is a healthy country. The tap water comes direct from the Highlands and is tastier than most and you should need no vaccinations or medication to travel here.

Scotland's free National Health Service has been keeping the population healthy for decades. Foreign visitors can also enjoy free treatment for medical emergencies and minor injuries (broken legs, etc). However, any treatment outside of accident and emergency is not covered and must be arranged with your travel insurer in advance.

Chapter 4:
About the Upcoming Destination Chapters

This guidebook divides Scotland into clear geographical chunks. Edinburgh and Glasgow have their own chapters and the rest is detailed based on typical travel routes. Under each chapter you'll find an introduction, a section on travel essentials, and then detailed information about the travel experiences to discover. Here's an overview:

Chapter 5: Edinburgh – Scotland's capital is also the premier attraction and entry point. Charming and atmospheric, it's a wonderful immersion in the old vibe of the country.

Chapter 6: Glasgow – Glasgow revels in being alternative and the experience is vastly different to that in Edinburgh, despite the cities being barely an hour apart. Ignore the rough looking facade, Glasgow is intriguing, alternative, and an essential part of an itinerary.

Chapter 7: The Central Belt – In and around Glasgow and Edinburgh, the Central Belt destinations are easy as day trips from a base in either of the cities. While this is Scotland's urban heart, it's still dominated by brilliant displays of green space and cute village attractions.

Chapter 8: Southern Scotland – Sandwiched between England and the Central Belt, this is an area of rural villages, remnants of medieval war, and hills that roll beyond the horizon.

Chapter 9: North East Scotland – With a mesmerizing coastline on one side and the rugged Grampian Mountains to the other, North East Scotland is a sublime land of beaches, hiking, whisky, and iconic Scottish scenery.

Chapter 10: The Scottish Highlands and Islands – Running along the West Coast and continuing to the northern tip of Britain, the Highlands are Scotland at their most dramatic and untamed. Expect meandering country roads, mountains towering over fields of heather, and endless expanses of national park.
Three groups of islands scatter the Scottish coast, each offering a very traditional portrayal of Gaelic life and spectacular scenery. The Hebrides are off the North West Coast, Orkney Islands off the Northern tip, and Shetland

Islands stand isolated far to the north of the country. They're accessed via the Highlands.

Chapter 5:
Edinburgh

Edinburgh appears like a dream; the castle towering above rows of historic streets, heritage living on in a capital city, and plenty of tradition to enjoy. Shortbread, ginger wigs, tartan, strange fried meals; it's all here within moments of arriving. The city's history is a large part of its appeal, the ruins and relics filling most itineraries. But ultimately, Edinburgh is a relaxed and atmospheric city where visitors find intrigue everywhere, not just in the attractions charging entry tickets. Like most capitals, the prices of everything shoot up in Edinburgh, especially along the Royal Mile and anywhere within walking distance of the castle. However, it's rare to visit Scotland and not see Edinburgh, a place that's both a snapshot of Scotland and a city break of continual charm.

Edinburgh Castle viewed from the Royal Mile

Travel Essentials for Edinburgh

Getting Here: Edinburgh International Airport is the country's busiest and is the main entry point for visitors arriving in Scotland. From the airport, the Airport Express takes half an hour and drops you at Waverly Train Station in the center of Edinburgh. Waverly is the terminus for long-distance trains coming from across Scotland and London. Note that the Old Town was deliberately built on a hill so it would be hard to access. That was a challenging for invading armies and can be a challenge for tourists wheeling heavy luggage.

Getting Around: The old part of Edinburgh is small enough to negotiate on foot, just be prepared for the hills. Going further afield, a good suburban bus network connects destinations. From Edinburgh it's possible to find connections to most places in Scotland. Note that the narrow streets and busy traffic can make Edinburgh challenging if you're driving. It's probably quicker to leave the car at the hotel and go out on foot.

Planning an Itinerary: Two days is good to see the main attractions as detailed below. Four or more days enables you to cover the eclectic diversity of Edinburgh as well as take day trips into the surrounding urban belt.

Accommodation in Edinburgh: More expensive than elsewhere in Scotland with prices in the Old Town vastly inflated. Edinburgh is relatively small so there's no need to get a hotel underneath the castle. Most major hotel chains have an offering in central Edinburgh yet in the outlying suburbs you'll find the more personal guesthouses and bed and breakfasts.

Edinburgh Experiences

Edinburgh City Chambers

Edinburgh In Two Days

With a couple of days it's easy to base your time around the **Old Town** and its pantheon of attractions. Add in a couple of places in the **New Town** and two days will fly by quickly. With the hills and often inclement weather, cramming in more makes it more of a slog than a wander through enchantment. Note that it's not necessary to stay in the Old Town to enjoy it. From surrounding suburbs you're only usually 15-20 minutes bus ride away. To save time during the peak summer tourist season, buy your tickets online for the main attractions.

Old Town

- Located directly beside Waverly Train Station, the excellent **Visit Scotland Information Centre** is an ideal first stop. Pick up free maps, find out about current exhibitions and performances, and the friendly staff will book any tickets you need.

- The **Old Town** is dominated by **Edinburgh Castle**, a majestic fortress that imperiously stands over the city and has been in constant use for over 1000 years. It's still a working building and the castle's attractions are fragmented, including a variety of historic exhibits, great halls, and view points. Take the map when you enter and try plan a route before heading off aimlessly. The busiest attraction are the Scottish crown jewels: if there's a queue come back later.

- Beneath the castle, with dazzling views onto the looming stone above, **St. Cuthbert's Church** is Britain's oldest and is surprisingly missed by most tourists. Check out Agatha Christie's marriage certificate on display inside.

- Around the corner from the castle, the Greco Roman columns of the **Scottish National Gallery** glimpse at the opulence to discover inside. The art is classic in style – portraits, 16th century swirls of oil paint – but there's also a good section on Scottish artists. This is a free attraction.

- Edinburgh Old Town dates back to the medieval era and the streets are full of cobblestones and intrigue. Dissecting the narrow lanes is the **Royal Mile**, Scotland's most famous street and one that divides opinion. The shops and hotel fronts of the Royal Mile leave a bullying taste of over-commercialism. In one sense it's no different from any city high street. However, the buildings are wonderfully dated and the charm is impossible to disregard. In addition, leading off from the Royal Mile are **dozens of charming alleys and streets**, and it's here that the old glory of Edinburgh is preserved and celebrated. With the Royal Mile as the compass, it's easy to get lost while you wander. A few attractions jutting off the Royal Mile worth mentioning are:

- **Mary's King's Close** is a slice of medieval haunted curiosity. Untouched since it was closed over 300 years ago, it's the further you can get to stepping back in time.

- Edinburgh's historic city church is a peaceful place for an hour, especially when it's raining. **St Giles' Cathedral** has the blend of stained glass, towering archways, and whiffs of antiquity.

- **Greyfriars Kirkyard** is a spooky place and it's interesting to read the inscriptions on the tombs of famous Scots from down the centuries. Make sure you head into the church.

- **The Grassmarket area** helps to satisfy preconceptions of what a historic old town will look like. Instead of the major chains on the Royal Mile, this is a unique place of independent shops, cafes, bars, restaurants, and doorways you want to peek into. Best enjoyed towards dusk as you can check out the shops and then explore the bars.

- Head into **Gladstone's Land**, a 17th century tenement with an interior that's been preserved from this period. Another historic house worth entering is the **John Knox House Museum**, the original home of the man who had an affair with Mary Queen of Scots. Both these charge an entrance fee and it's not worth paying for more than one as they offer much of the same. **Lady Stair's House** is a further 17th century attraction. It's the least impressive but this one is free.

- Situated in the Lady Stair house is the **Writers' Museum**. It's an informative look at the strong history of Scottish literature, including Robert Burns, Robert Louis Stevenson, and Sir Walter Scott. Free entrance.

- Staring across from each other are two contrasting museums. **The Museum of Edinburgh** charts the city's history through displays of silver and random exhibits. Then the People's Story charts life - in all its horrors and challenges – of the city's 18th century inhabitants. Both are free.

- Numerous companies offer **free Edinburgh walking tours**. Free that is, as long as you offer a tip. These do breathe life and chronicles into the different parts of the Old Town. You'll see their adverts up around the Old Town.

- The Royal Mile connects the castle with **Holyroodhouse Abbey and Palace.** The official residence of the Queen comes with the kind of pomp and razzmatazz you would expect from Mrs Elizabeth II. Some of the palace is open to the public, including the grand Queen's Gallery, containing an eclectic mix of famous international art.

New Town

- Edinburgh's age is epitomized by the Georgian townhouses of the **New Town**. Most of this area dates to the late 18th century and it's equally charming and grandiose to explore. The New Town hasn't been preserved like the Old Town, so when the houses crumble they're often replaced with a strange concrete monstrosity. Still, it's well worth a look around and the historic townhouses easily rival those found in London or Bath.

- An absolutely bizarre structure of modernity in the New Town, the **Scottish Parliament** is regarded as en eyesore by most locals. Some people are impressed with the ingenuity though. You can watch parliament in session by organizing tickets online in advance, for free.

- For chill time, especially when the sun is shining, head to **Prince's Street Gardens**, a vast expanse of green in the center of the city. It's particularly impressive in fall when leaves fall and cover the pathways in red and orange.

- If you don't fancy the walk up Arthur's Seat (see below) then excellent views of old Edinburgh can be found from the top of the gothic spire in **Scott Monument**, on the edge of Prince's Street Gardens.

- Containing exhibits and artifacts from everything Scottish, the **National Museum of Scotland** is a free and very interesting place to spend most of a rainy day.

- This city of hills has many potential viewpoints for your two days in the city. Perhaps the closest and easiest for anyone short on time is **Carlton Hill**. From here, the iconic monuments roll towards an often misty horizon.

Edinburgh in Four Days or More

Spend more time and the other suburbs become the scenes for days of exploring. These experiences don't spill into each other like those in the Old Town, however, with four days it's easy to cross the city and take in a few of these attractions.

Historic Attractions

- The best views over Edinburgh come from **Arthur's Seat**, one of the four hills that the city is built upon. The remains here date back over 2000 years and can be poignant reminders of the city's ancient history. The ascending climb can be slippy, especially when the rocks are slippy after the rain. However, it's not as challenging - or as long - as the locals make out.

- Another out of town fortress in ruins is **Craigmillar Castle**, dating from the 14th century and without the crowds of Arthur's Seat. It has none of the Edinburgh Castle crowds and is a wonderful look at a medieval era. Highly recommended.

- More of a stately home than a fortress, **Lauriston Castle** looks like it's even too grand for Downton Abbey. Built with local stone and peppered with chimneys, it could also be a setting for a Harry Potter film. Indelibly beautiful, Lauriston is free to visit from the outside. Heading inside is only possible on 2pm tours running Sunday to

Thursday. It's the kind of place for taking photos that have friends clambering with jealousy.

- Just outside Edinburgh, the weird subterranean chambers of **Gilmerton Cove** reveal weird and wonderful things that exist beneath the city.

Exploring the City

- The **Water of Leith Walkway** is a network of walking trails and cycle paths, exploring and connecting large parts of off the beaten track Edinburgh. Maps are available from the Visit Scotland office and it's easy to jump on and off the trail as you discover the diversity of the city.

- Perhaps the finest stop on the Leith Walkway is **Dean Village**, a succession of mils and stone bridges that feel like the old-world in a nutshell.

- Dominating the Leith harbor and as glorious a ship you'll find anywhere in the world, the **Royal Yacht Britannia** is the queen's floating palace. Despite its size, it does get crowded with tourist hoards exploring the ostentatious rooms. For a more relaxed (and more expensive) visit, book a table and enjoy the original 'high tea' experience on board.

- Next to the yacht, the **Ocean Terminal** shopping mall has a huge selection of cafes and cheap eats if the weather turns.

- The whole waterfront around Leith is one of the city's most enchanting areas. Known as **The Shore**, it's an area of stained glass windows, art boutiques, and plenty of hidden pubs with an excellent gastro grub.

Galleries and Gardens

- Art fans will find a more Scottish flavor in the exhibitions in the **Scottish National Gallery of Modern Art**.

- Housed in a more impressive building and focusing on traditional portraits from the ages, the **Scottish National Portrait Gallery** is another free attraction worth visiting.

- When the sun is shining, the **Royal Botanic Garden** is a good free place for a picnic. Avoid when it's raining as everyone crowds into the glasshouses, filling them with condensation and muggy air.

- A more impressive garden attraction is **Jupiter Artland**, a mass of sculptures, art installations, and curved expanses of cultivated green. Very peaceful and blossoming beneath choruses of birdsong.

More to Discover in Edinburgh

- Scotland might not have the English Premier League but its sport scene has a wonderfully local atmosphere. The city's two main football teams, **Hearts** and **Hibernian**, have feisty atmospheres that get the pulse raising. **Murrayfield** is the national stadium and if you visit in spring, there's a chance of watching a 6 Nations rugby match between Scotland and one of its UK rivals.

- **The Edinburgh Dungeon** is like most dungeon attractions around the world. It is spooky. But it's very expensive and hardly reflects the character of the city.

- **The Scotch Whisky Experience** offers a ride through the whisky making process along with the chance to sample hundreds of whiskeys. However, note that most of what you're sampling is overpriced.

Edinburgh's August Festivals

During August the city rolls with the drama and delight of half a dozen festivals that run practically simultaneously. This is easily the most expensive and touristic time to visit Edinburgh. But if you don't mind the crowds, it's also the most interesting.

- One of the world's most famous cultural festivals takes place every August in the city. **The Edinburgh Fringe** is part subculture, part avant-garde, and part mass celebration of the arts. Venues all over the city offer plays, comedy, live music, and peculiar offbeat programs. This is the world's biggest arts festival and is a sea of color and expressionism.

- **The Edge Festival** is the commercialized music festival running off the back of the Fringe. There's nothing original here. Expect pop acts and screaming families.

- Scotland and Edinburgh have a fine record in spawning cutting edge authors that pull no punches. The **Edinburgh International Book Festival** is one of the world's best, and it stays a million miles away from anything you might find on the three for two aisles at the airport.

- Before the Fringe, and often sited as the reason the Fringe developed, the **Edinburgh International Festival** involves varied shows of opera and theater. Over the years, the prices have come down to Fringe levels and the festival has become less high-brow.

- A more local festival feel is enjoyed at the **Edinburgh Mela**, taking place in Leith and usually consisting of heavy drinking in the Leith pubs.

- There are few more iconic sights that watching a thousand men in kilts belting out tunes on the bagpipes. The **Edinburgh Military Tattoo**, taking place beneath Edinburgh Castle, is a mass parade of royal Scottishness and ancient tradition. Tickets sell out months in advance but touts on the streets sell them on for inflated prices.

The Best Places to Eat and Drink in Edinburgh

The following represents a varied selection of the finest places to dine and drink in the Scottish capital. It's not intended to be comprehensive, but to offer a few exceptional places to consider.

- The Scots are enthusiastic bakers. Most locals will claim that their grandma does the best scones and cakes in the world. **Mimi's Bakehouse** is one of the places that challenges home cooking and it's been a previous winner of the Scottish Baker of the Year award.

- Surprisingly, the tradition of the tea house and high tea is rapidly disappearing from the UK. In can still be savored in an iconic setting at **Anteaques**.

- To splurge in royal surroundings, get a table at the **Cafe Royal Circle Bar.** It's not cheap but the ambiance rewards the wallet.

- **Waters of Leith Cafe Bistro** offers great value food in the Leith area, with fabulous views and a range of dishes.

- The **Grassmarket area** of the Old Town has lots of classic old pubs. While they're overpriced, they offer a great iconic pub reverie for first time visitors to the UK. Pubs and drinking are a local obsession and you'll find them all over the city. The squalid looking ones are usually atmospheric and welcoming once you're inside. They're just scary from the outside. The nicer looking pubs are the places for cheap and good traditional food. In particular, check out **Pickles** and **Blackfriars**.

- Scotland is the world's home of whisky and the choice on offer can be baffling to first timers. For a broad introduction to Scottish whisky, visit the **Scotch Whisky Heritage Centre** and don't be shy about your lack of knowledge.

Chapter 6:
Glasgow

Glasgow and Edinburgh: two Scottish cities less than an hour apart that could hardly be more different. Glasgow is the creative and economic hub of Scotland, a city that's been regenerated from industrial decline to thriving epitome of all that's great about Scotland. A vibrant music scene was rewarded as it was named a UNESCO City of Music. It's also a UNESCO Creative City and was an early holder of European City of Culture.

Glasgow takes the Scottish traits of friendliness and tradition, and blends them into a package that spans the centuries and rewards anyone with time. Pub chatter emanates across streets that juxtapose Edwardian townhouses with sparkling modern architecture. Breweries and distilleries litter valleys of green that surround the city. Victorian attractions are followed by a night at the theater, or a day shopping until the feet complain and a cosy restaurant provides solace.

Glasgow at night

Travel Essentials for Glasgow

Getting Here: Glasgow Airport is actually in Ayrshire and a good 50kms from the city center. It's an airport hub for Ryanair and that means cheap flights from many destinations in Europe. The airport has a railway station with twice hourly trains to the center: show your boarding pass to get a half price ticket (around £4). It's quicker than taking the bus. Edinburgh Airport is only a little further away and there are direct buses to Glasgow from here. Central Station has trains arriving from anywhere south, including London. Queen Street Station is the terminus if you're coming from Northern Scotland. Bus services arrive at Buchanan Bus Station. All three are within reasonable distance to most of Glasgow city center.

For day trippers, there are countless trains and buses that move between Edinburgh and Glasgow. These trains take one of four routes and the price is always the same. So choose a CrossCountry or ScotRail Shuttle rather than the slower Scotrail services via Motherwell.

Getting Around: Hosting the 2014 Commonwealth Games helped to improve an already impressive transport infrastructure and getting around is easy. Despite being Scotland's biggest city, there's only 600,000 inhabitants, so there's no long slogs on buses. In addition, Glaswegians are fiercely proud and asking for directions or advice usually gives them a glow of identity. Glasgow is a pedestrian friendly city and most of the major central streets are closed to traffic.

A one line subway runs in a loop around the city center on both sides of the River Clyde. The £4 unlimited day travel ticket makes this a great option. Buses go pretty much everywhere in the city, although it's worth asking advice before jumping on board. Buses to the same destination can take very different lengths of time as some literally go around the houses and take longer than walking.

Planning an Itinerary: The dilemma when planning a Glasgow visit is how much time to devote to the city. Is this going to be a one day charge around the city's attractions? Or a three day immersion in the fascinating range of experiences. Both options are included below.

Accommodation in Glasgow: Hotel prices make Glasgow a cheaper alternative to Edinburgh as a base to for exploring Scotland. There's no single suburb that's most popular but anywhere on the subway line makes for easy getting around and exploring. Like the city, the accommodation is a real mishmash of ideas and tradition. Modern city hotels can be found at excellent prices during low season while historic looking bed and breakfasts offer a more four poster and black pudding experience.

Glasgow Experiences

In One Day

One day is only enough to glimpse and scratch the surface of the city. However, this option has been included here because many people visit Glasgow as part of a day trip from Edinburgh. If you have time, it's highly recommended to stay in both major cities and really absorb the different vibes. If you only have a day, here's what not to miss.

- Glasgow flourished in the 19th and early 20th century. The legacy to this wealth lies in the **stone carved Victorian and Edwardian buildings** scattered across the center of town. Built from red and blonde sandstone, they're particularly resplendent when the sun leaves dusk glows across their exteriors. Unfortunately, many of these buildings were torn down and replaced by concrete monstrosities between the fifties and seventies. These in turn have now been torn down as the city realizes the mistake. The surviving traditional buildings are a core attraction. Check out:

    - Over 1600 years old and dazzling in its gothic style, the **Glasgow Cathedral** is free to enter. It's worth taking a peak inside just for the huge arched ceiling and intricate design.

    - Around **George Square** are numerous statues of local luminaries, each of them looking across to the **City Chambers**, headquarters for the local government and a timeless photo of Renaissance architecture. George Square always has a bustling upbeat vibe that compliments the architecture.

George Square

- o Europe's largest public library, **Mitchell Library** is housed in a majestic Edwardian building with corridors leading into seemingly hundreds of rooms. It's easy to get lost here.

- o Another free building that offers a look at the interiors of these old buildings is the **Scotland Street School**. It focus is the design of Charles Rennie Mackintosh, an integral figure in the development of the city.

- o Most middle class Glaswegians once lived in three or four stories tenement houses. It was these that the council tore down in the fifties. **Tenement House** recreates the early 20th century and is an excellent attraction.

- Scotland's most visited attraction is the **Kelvingrove Art Gallery and Museum**, a veritable treasure trove of exhibits that span the centuries and shimmer beneath opulent ceilings. There's are a variety of wings; some are where you'll find WWII bombers and medieval armor, others are where Dali and Van Gogh originals shine. Kelvingrove is huge and – unless you can manage the four hours plus to see it all – it's worth consulting the map and planning your route to take in what's of most interest.

- **Buchanan Street** is Glasgow's core street and buzzes with the music of street performers.

- Running through the heart of the city are vast streets of shops and shopping arcades. You can't miss them, like the **Buchanan Galleries** and **St Enoch Centre,** officially the largest glass roofed building in Europe. More boutique and prestigiously expensive, the **Argyle Arcade** is packed with jewelry stores. Designer indulgence is found in **Princes Square**, a very upmarket mall to take the credit card.

- Filling the rooms of a glorious 18th century mansion, the **Gallery of Modern Art** features a collection of the best Scottish artists. It's best for the building though; Corinthian columns, stained glass, gloriously carved ceilings etc.

With Three Days or More

Now Glasgow comes alive. Live music gigs, funky arcades, exploring Edwardian streets that twinkle with offbeat treats...Glasgow's immersion is an iconic one. While it's attractions don't have the same must-see pull of Edinburgh, get to know the city and it's perhaps the most interesting in the whole of the UK.

Art and Museums

- In the heart of the city on Buchanan Street you'll find the **Visit Scotland Information Centre**. The staff are famously helpful and will help plan a public transport route to take you around the different attractions in and outside Glasgow.

- The city's art scene is centered around the **Scottish Exhibition and Conference Centre Complex**. There's always more than one thing going on here, from opera performances in the **Clyde Auditorium** to exhibitions that showcase post-modern local artists.

- **Glasgow University** looks like a British postcard, the lawns neatly manicured as they lead onto 19th century buildings. There's a visitor's centre in the main building (this is actually the UK's fourth oldest university) with great views over the city.

- Within the university complex you'll find the **Hunterian Museum and Art Gallery**, also free, and worth a visit for the building interior as much as the exhibits. There's a very famous Whistler collection here. This museum is actually spread over four different venues and it's good to pick one or two. **Hunterian Art Gallery, Mackintosh House** (for Glasgow history), **Anatomy Museum**, and the **Zoology Museum**. All are glorious buildings.

- In a peculiar building, the **Glasgow School or Art** has many exhibits on contemporary art. Some will love it, others will wonder how the definitions of art have changed so much since oil portraits.

- Glasgow contains a number of free museums that make for interesting hours in the city. While none are award winning, they're all worthy places for a rainy day. Try the **Glasgow Police Museum** and its paraphernalia of stories; the **Burrell Collection** with over 9,000 pieces of art; the **Riverside Museum** and its sampling of locomotives and buses from 100 years ago; and **Transmission Gallery**, a funky hub for ex-student artists.

In the Evenings

- Glasgow has scores of **concert halls and drama spaces** with more agreeable prices than those in Edinburgh. An evening at the ballet or theater blends live performance with world renowned venues. Visit Scotland have flyers and information on current performances and can book tickets. The most impressive of the venues are: the **Panopticon Music Hall** (the oldest music hall in the world), with its velvety interior; **Citizens Theatre,** which has launched the careers of hundreds of movie stars; **Glasgow Royal Concert Hall,** which plays host to traditional symphonic and Scottish music; and **Kings Theatre**, the city's largest and grandest performing space.

- For a completely different night out, Glasgow has one of the Europe's most cutting edge underground electronic music scenes. Clubs like the **Arches** and the **Sub Club** throb with pounding techno music and ceilings that drip with the sweat from packed revelers.

- For a rather drunken yet illuminating journey through Glasgow, do the **Subcrawl**, stopping at each metro stop and dipping into a local pub for a drink. There's 15 stops, so pace yourself.

Places to Relax and Explore

- With just one day you'll be touring the **West End** area ticking off the famous buildings. With more time this is place to get lost, especially in the early evenings when the bars begin to hum with life.

- Glasgow is proud of having more parkland than any other British city. Four potential city parks are easy spaces to hang out during the summer months. The grandest are the **gardens at Kelvingrove Art Gallery and Museum**, with the most diverse being the **Botanic Gardens** (note the sublime **Kibble Palace** to visit beside the gardens). Locals tend to prefer **Glasgow Green**, a vast open space ignited by live concerts during summer evening. **Tollcross Park** takes away the prize as most impressive, it's cultivated pathways running past rose gardens, nature walks, and hedge mazes.

- Just outside the city and deserving a special entry, **Pollok Country Park** is a place of grazing highland cattle, woods, and a vast mansion. There's a cute tearoom for refueling if you visit in winter. **Linn Park** is staggeringly pretty in fall, when deep tones of red cover the arched bridges as leaves fall from the woodland.

- Glasgow's atmospheric marketplace and purveyor of fun, **the Barras** is where everything from the back of a lorry swamps stalls of bargains. It's working class Glasgow at its soulful best and a great people watching spot. Stop for a super cheap lunch of fried fish and chips in one of the many cafes around here.

- For the best views of the city, the surreal **Necropolis** is a mass cemetery of elaborate tombs and Celtic crosses rising towards the sky.

- Late afternoons throb with life in **Merchant City**, the former district of Glasgow merchants that's seen a revival of sorts in the last decade. Come to hang out, have a drink, and try some hip restaurants.

Something Different

- Glasgow is a city divided by football and elevated by religion. Glasgow Celtic (Catholic) and Glasgow Rangers (Protestant) have one of the fiercest rivalries in world football and their **Old Firm Derby** is not for the feint-hearted. There's real hatred on the streets and sporadic violence breaks out around the stadiums. Both teams have 50,000 plus capacity stadiums that are packed out on match days (during the season, one but not the other team will be playing at home). The atmosphere at these games is usually more impressive than watching a football game in England. Both venues also have **stadium tours**.

- Another football experience can be found in the **Scottish Football Museum**, which loves to poke fun of the English and the Scots victories over their rivals.

- **Tennents** is Scotland's largest and most popular brewer, and their brewery can fill a rainy afternoon with drunkenness.

- A slightly more highbrow but equally drunk day can be spent at **Glengoyne Distillery**, where barrels stand proud in vast chambers. It's a captivating setting although that might be the whisky talking.

Where to Eat and Drink in Glasgow

- **Willow Tea Rooms** is perhaps Scotland's most sublime, housed in various rooms restored to their early 20th century pomp. **The Corinthian** is equally beautiful yet a little pompous. You can imagine the Queen sampling her cucumber sandwiches here.

- A furnisher of iconic Scottish food, **The Ubiquitous Chip** is where to go for gourmet haggis and all those weird meals in your preconceptions.

- Gordon Ramsey is Scotland's most famous chef and his former partner in crime, Briane Maule, runs what's widely regarded as the finest restaurant in Glasgow. The **Chardon D'Or** is expensive but atmospheric with regular live music.

- Truly eclectic and next to the Buchanan Street Shops, the **Market Kitchen Glasgow** offers fine dining at a great price.

- Hundreds upon hundreds of take aways line the streets and they're just about as unhealthy as you can get. However...they serve the country's infamous and essential-to-try **deep fried Mars Bar**. Don't expect it to taste good and you'll probably end up feeling sick: it's a deep fried Mars Bar after all.

- Nattering away in a local pub is the core social life of most Glaswegians. You'll find thousands of pubs in the city, with four distinct areas worth considering for either a quick pint or a night out. The **West End** offers the most upmarket options; **Merchant City** is a mix of dive bars and swanky places; **Sauchiehall Street** is a more localized and traditional place to drink; and **South Side** is becoming a cross of working class roots with burgeoning bohemia. In all these places you'll have dozens of pubs within walking distance.

- Opposite Kelvingrove Museum, **BrewDog Glasgow** allows you taste a full range of Scottish ales, each slowly hand pulled from the many taps along the bar.

- If your whisky knowledge isn't up to scratch then visit **Oran Mor** or **The Pot Still**. The bar staff will talk you through the options until you fall off the barstool in inebriated bliss.

Chapter 7:
The Central Belt

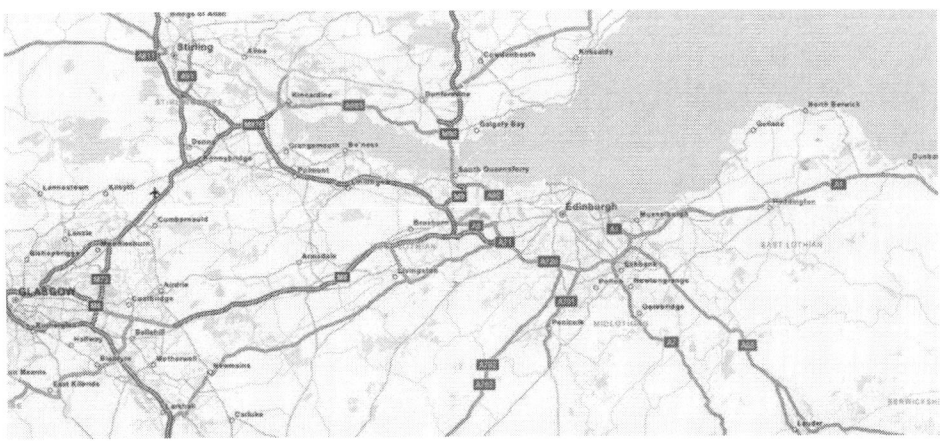

Scotland's urban heart is found in a narrow strip of land in and around Edinburgh and Glasgow. Attractions are nestled between the two major cities, as well as spilling out onto the rolling hills that surround the major cities. This is an area of surprise: 9th century chapels emerge in forests, quaint villages offer an easy escape from the city, and there's always a panorama when the road ascends. The experiences and destinations here are usually visited as day trips from a Glasgow or Edinburgh base, but for those preferring tranquility, some of the villages listed could be a base from which to visit the city for a day. Note that Edinburgh and Glasgow are the main destinations and cities in the Central Belt but are featured extensively in chapters five and six.

Travel Essentials for the Central Belt

- **Getting Here:** Almost invariably, visiting any of the destinations listed below starts in Glasgow or Edinburgh. Both cities have extensive travel connections and you'll usually be traveling by bus.

- **Getting Around:** Sporadic rural buses connect some of the more far flung areas and you'll always be able to get by with public transport, so long as you don't mind a wait.

- **Planning an Itinerary:** Visitors usually pick one or two of these destinations as day trips from the city. With a rental car it's also easy to visit a hearty handful of the places below in a day.

- **Accommodation in the Central Belt:** Far cheaper and cuter than its city rivals, there's some excellent bargains to be had in this part of Scotland. Some may even prefer to stay in villages like Dunbar or North Berwich and then day trip to Edinburgh.

Central Belt Experiences

Itinerary Planning

From a traveler's perspective, the Central Belt can be split into three geographic regions. Edinburgh sits at the heart of the Lothians, while Glasgow is in Clydeside. The area of Stirlingshire stands north of the two.

This is a region that struggles to claim much time in visitor's itineraries. With one day, you can choose a handful of destinations in either of these three regions. With more time, it's possible to dedicate a day to each. Getting out into one of these areas is particularly recommended if you don't plan to travel to Northeast Scotland or the Scottish Highlands.

Stirlingshire (accessed from Glasgow and Edinburgh)

Starting north of the motorway between the two cities, Stirlingshire is a major destination in its own right. This area is the most inherently attractive of the three to use as a base and a place to spend a few days exploring.

- **Loch Lomand and the Trossachs National Park** marks the start of the Scottish Highlands (see Chapter 10). For those short on time, it's an easy and sublime immersion in precipitous slopes of sheep, castles lost in the middle of nowhere, and scenery that fulfills all preconceptions of Scotland. Hourly trains head from Glasgow to the excellent **visitors center at Balloch**. Some staggering hiking trails and the main attraction, with the **West Highland Trail to Fort William** a challenging yet iconic journey into the highlands of Scotland. Sightseeing trips can be done by passenger ferry across the loch, or by taking any local bus that weaves slowly through the national park.

- As it rolls north, Loch Lomand blurs into **Queen Elizabeth Forest Park**, another great expanse of green hiking trails and astonishing panoramas. The visitors centre at **Aberfoyle** is relatively easy to reach.

- Built upon volcanic rock and oozing both medieval and Renaissance buildings, **Stirling** is a proud utopia of all Scotland stands for. **The Stirling Castle** is one of Scotland's finest attractions, not only an impressive building but an evocative history lesson of war and battle. The town is an excellent and more local alternative to staying in Glasgow or Edinburgh and is less than an hour by bus or train to the two cities.

Stirling Castle

- Just north of Stirling, an eclectic group of attractions can easily fill a full day. The most common combination is to explore **Doune Castle** in the morning before spending the afternoon tasting whisky at **Deanstone Visitors Centre**.

- While Falkirk sometimes looks rough, it's a town of history and a couple of attractions on different compass points. The **Falkirk Wheel** is the world's only rotating boat lift and there are nice boat trips starting from here. Built with turf and somehow surviving for 1900 years, the **Antonine Wall** is a good alternative to the longer day trip down to **Hadrians Wall**. It's dotted with roman forts that rise through the hills.

- Stirlingshire has been the scene of **countless battles between Scotland and invading English armies**. If you've seen the movie Braveheart, then you'll have an idea of the bloodshed. Tour companies from Falkirk and Stirling run excellent tours to these fields of green and breathe life into the battles.

Lothian (Accessed from Edinburgh)

Stretching out to a rolling coastline, Lothian is a mishmash of quaint villages and working class neighborhoods with plenty of charm.

- Made famous by The Da Vinchi Code, **Rosslyn Chapel** is an enchanting stop less than 30 minutes by bus from Central Edinburgh. Situated in a quintessentially Scottish village, the chapel radiates elaborate and intricate design and looks ever bit like a potential movie set.

- The history of Scotland's mines and coal industry is explored at the **National Mining Museum of Scotland** in **Newtongrange**. There's a scarcely veiled attack on the British Conservative government of the seventies that's amusing to read about.

- As the A1 winds east it cuts through villages that feature little more than a closed down post office and a pub. One that's definitely worth the bus ride is **Pencaitland**, where the royal splendor of **Winton Estate** is set in vast gardens that vociferously scream of *Downton Abbey*.

- Take the A1 further out of Edinburgh (note you're still less than an hour from the capital here), and the huge **St Mary's Church in Haddington** makes for a recommended stop. There's the ideal blend of old stone grandeur with humble village to explore. A few miles further along you reach the crumbling remains of **Hailes Castle**, a place that immediately evokes images of medieval war between Scotland and England. **East Linton** is the next village along the A1 and its traditional pubs and high street are worth exploring.

- Close to East Linton, the **National Museum of Flight** has five hangars filled with planes from the annals of history. WWII bombers are interesting but the Concorde exhibition is what justifies the entrance ticket.

- Coastal **Dunbar** is still only an hour from Edinburgh and it's an absolute gem of a fisher village, full of old white stone houses and fish fumes. Bring your warm coat and wander around with a warm fish and chip packet in your hands.

- Rather than take the A1, a road out of Edinburgh skirts the coast on its way to **North Berwick** and two wonderful castles. **Dirleton Castle and Gardens** is less visited but hypnotically ruined, while **Tantallon Castle** imperiously stands over the North Sea's foamy waves. On a warm day, nearby **Seacliffe Beach** adds another stop to the day trip.

- West of Edinburgh, **Linlithgow** is the most popular day trip. The narrow old village makes for a nice wander before exploring the stunning ruins of **Linlithgow Palace**, acres of fascinating stone standing beside a loch. While in the town, **Annet House Museum** charts local history and epitomizes the cuteness of the village. Within walking distance of the town are three other attractions. **St. Michael's Parish Church** is peaceful and imposingly grand, the **House of the Binns** is a glimpse at old money, and **Linlithgow Canal Centre** makes for a serene stop for a mug of tea.

Clydeside (accessed from Glasgow)

This side of the Central Belt is more built up than Lothian but there's still some easy day trips to iconic Scotland, especially when you head southeast from the city.

- **Hamilton** isn't the most attractive of towns but it's worth exploring for **Chatelherault**, a humble yet alluring castle with peaceful gardens.

- Explorer and Christian pilgrim David Livingstone is somewhat of a local legend and chronicles of his missions through Africa are well presented at the **David Livingstone Centre** in **Blantyre**.

- **East Kilbride** has three attractions but best for those with their own transport. The **National Museum of Rural Life** charts Scottish villages through the centuries, while **Calderglen Country Park** and **James Hamilton Heritage Park** are good on a clear day.

- Barely 20 minutes from Glasgow, the intoxicating pub town of **Paisely** hides a long history. Visit Paisley Abbey, one of the finest in the whole country, as well as **Thomas Coats Memorial Baptist Church**, an ancient building that dominates a high street of countless pubs and men slurring their words.

Chapter 8:
Southern Scotland

Southern Scotland is hugely overlooked by visitors, yet it has the untrammeled charm to compel anyone. The wide green landscape is usually rushed through as people arrive from England, or missed as visitors prefer the more dramatic Highlands. However, visit the Scottish Borders and South West Scotland and you find an area of indelibly Scottish feel, with historic forts and abbeys dominating the itinerary.

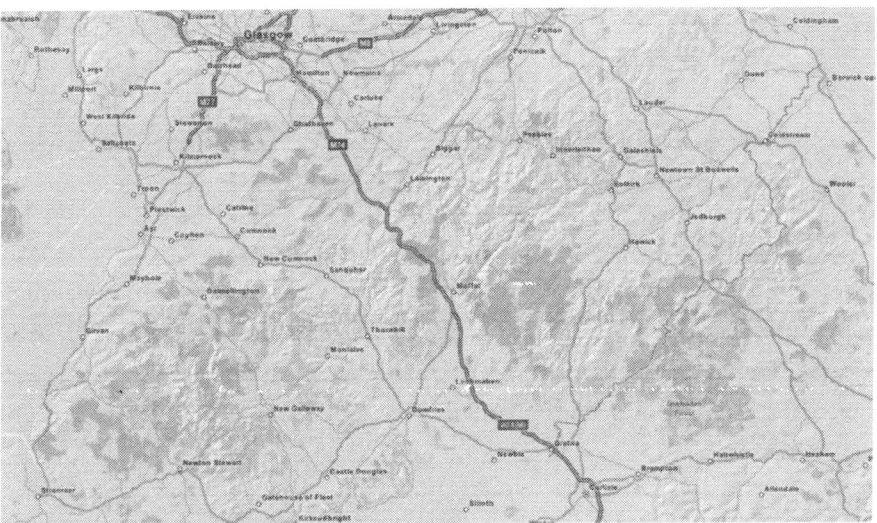

Travel Essentials for Southern Scotland

Getting Here: Most people will take public transport from Edinburgh or Glasgow. The alternative is to stop in Southern Scotland when coming from England, further to the south.

Getting Around: Part of Southern Scotland's lack of tourists can be explained by the limited public transport options. Trains and buses run to most destinations but the beauty of the area is usually found in what lies between, and you can't stop and admire it without your own transport.

Planning an Itinerary: Southern Scotland is split into two geographic area. The Scottish Borders that cover the southeastern half and the region of South West Scotland. With a tour or your own transport it's possible to explore either of these regions as day trips from Edinburgh or Glasgow. For those with more time, the Scottish Borders has a conglomeration of villages that are within easy reach of each other.

Accommodation in Southern Scotland: Due to the lack of visitors, you won't find any five star options here. However, the guesthouses and family run bed and breakfasts are the best value you'll find in Scotland (if not the whole UK).

Southern Scotland Experiences

Southern Scotland is divided into its eastern (the Borders) and western halves. With one day, it's a choice of picking a side and trying to explore as much as possible. But there are no time restrictions here. This could be a place to settle in, relax, and soak up rural Scottish life in its evocative glory.

The Scottish Borders

Dominated by soft greens and faded reds, the Scottish Borders is a rural area of scenery that makes the eyes smile. Edinburgh tour companies offer long day trips through the Borders region and it's eminently possible to visit all of the places below on a long day trip with your own transport. An another option is to base yourself in one of the abbey villages below. The following are listed in a southerly direction from Edinburgh.

- Most people skip through **Peebles** and **Innerleithen** but they seem to epitomize the classic appeal of Scotland. There's a castle in ruins (**Neidpath**), a rugged piece of hilly forest (**Glentress**), and enough local pubs to keep you stocked in stout and black pudding for a decade (Innerleithen).

- A cluster of small villages beside the A7 offer a look at both working class and regal Scotland. Come for the historic markets, old stone bridges, and stately homes, as well as the splendid abbeys.

    - **Galashiels** and **Abbotsford** is the site of **Abbotsford House**, as fine an example of opulent royalty as anywhere in the country. Abbotsford village is the home of Sir Walter Scott and everything in the village seems to remind you of this fact.

    - **Earlston** has its own version, **Mellerstain House**.

Melrose Abbey

- Historic **Melrose Abbey** is a dazzling ruin on a huge scale and the most visited of attractions in the Scottish Borders. Allow a couple of hours to really submerge yourself in the masonry and history. A stone cross marks where the heart of Robert the Bruce is buried while narrow winding stairs take you to top of the Abbey.

- Only 15 miles further east, **Kelso Abbey** isn't as big or as well maintained, but it's nonetheless impressive. If it wasn't for nearby Melrose, Kelso Abbey would surely have a far higher tourist profile.

- Further south, as you get within 15 miles of the border, lie the villages of Jedburgh and Harwick. **Harwick** is the nicer of the two but lacks attractions: unless you count people watching from a pub bench and markets of pensioners pushing tartan trolleys. **Jedburgh Abbey** is wonderfully photogenic with its succession of archways, and it's only walking distance to **Mary Queen of Scots House**, a stone carved historic building that charts the fascinating story of Mary. Also in town is the **Jedburgh Castle and Jail Museum**, a great choice for keeping kids entertained when considering the different ruins and castles around the country.

- **Hadrian's Wall**, the ancient stone divide between Scotland and England, is actually south of the border. Much of it was looted by peasants and farmers to build houses. Tour companies usually incorporate the wall into a Scottish Borders tour.

Southwest Scotland

- Rather inexplicably, this is Scotland's least visited county. Certainly by foreigners at least: the Scots are regular visitors here. A wild cliff lined coast is dotted with castles and cute bays while the inland road winds indelibly slowly through forests and curved expanses of misty countryside. Essentially there are two main routes, one taking the coastal road from Glasgow, and the other taking inland rural roads, also from Glasgow.

- The coastal route is easy to navigate by public transport as you head south and connect:

  - **Troon** is a delightful seaside village famous for its golf course (that will host the 2016 Open, one of the world's premier tournaments). Surrounded by billowing hills and filled with excellent seafood eateries, it makes for a serene day trip from Glasgow.

Troon

  - Ten miles further south you reach **Ayr**, birthplace of the poet Robert Burns and filled with a sprinkling of competing attractions. **Robert Burns Birthplace Museum** and **Burns Monument and Gardens** have somewhat of a niche audience as they present pouring adoration for the town's famous son. For none literary lovers, **Burns National Heritage Park** is housed in a converted 19th century building with endearing thatched roof.

- Ten miles east of Ayr, **Dumfries House** is another of Scotland's imposing stately homes. Counteract the grandeur by walking to nearby Cumnock Village and joining the locals in the high street pubs.

- This coastline is rough and ready, battered by howling winds yet beautiful in its own peculiar way. Part eroded by these winds, **Culzean Castle** stands as a sentry along the Scottish coast, its turrets gazing onto crashing seas and its wall slowly sinking into the earth. Many Scottish will say that this is their favorite castle in the whole country and it's hard to argue with this.

- These attractions can connect with the inland attractions below, forming a one to three day loop from Glasgow. The road crosses either due north or south of **Galloway Forest Park,** an attraction to consider for keen hikers and mountain bikers.

- This inland route isn't as clear cut and connecting the destinations without your own transport can be challenging:

  - Set in 80,000 acres of country park, **Drumlanrig Castle** looks something like a setting for a period drama. Imposing and inspiring, it's less than an hour from Glasgow.

  - In comparison, **Caerlaverock Castle** looks like its straight from some 15th century painting, the cultivated lawns running to a moat and standing before the iconic portrait of medieval ruins. It's nowhere near as big as Drumlanrig or Culzean but it's an unforgettable photo. Just across the river, on the A710, **Sweetheart Abbey** is, unsurprisingly, where you find couples taking selfies.

  - **Loch Ken** at **Castle Douglas** epitomizes the tranquility of southern Scotland. Come on a summer day and take a boat across waters flanked by forest.

- Sample the whisky of **Bladnoch Distillery**, a place of large barrels that lead to afternoon debauchery. **Annandale Distillery** isn't as famous for its produce but has a great cafe to spend the afternoon.

- Go back in time and explore the rather gaudy interior of **Broughton House** in **Kirkcudbright**, stuffed with Roman pillars, carved wood, and elaborate carpets.

- Dumfries town has been enthusiastically trying to tempt tourists to the southern reaches of Scotland. Housed in a peculiar cylindrical white tower, the **Dumfries Museum** excellently unveils the history of the region. **Robert Burns House** is where the poet spent his final days but it can be overkill if you've already stopped in Ayr.

Chapter 9:
North East Scotland

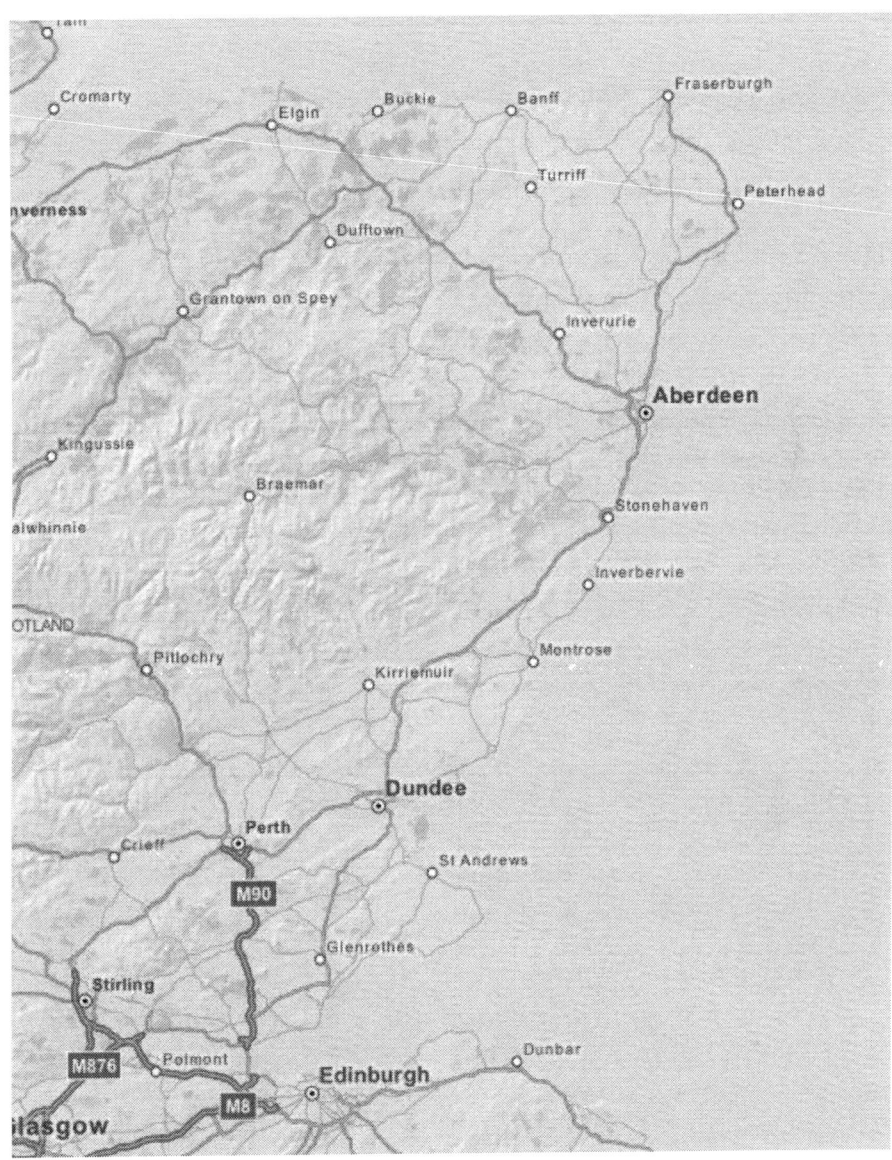

Preconceptions of Scotland come alive in North East Scotland. The Grampian Mountains form the western boundaries, cragged and seemingly impenetrable with their expanses of sheep filled land and forest. To the east lies an equally craggy coastline, home to some Europe's finest beaches and Scotland's most picturesque villages. Between these boundaries are many intriguing villages, most of them easily accessible. North East Scotland is also home to the country's whisky industry and the days can blur into weeks as hundreds of single malts are available to sample.

Travel Essentials for North East Scotland

Getting Here: Easily accessible from Glasgow, Edinburgh, or Stirling in the Central Belt. Much of the region's appeal is its accessibility, particularly when compared to the Scottish Highlands.

Getting Around: Public transport connections are good here, thanks to the myriad of decent sized towns and surprisingly lack of geological challenges. It's not necessary to have your own wheels to explore, other than when you go to the far north of the region.

Planning an Itinerary: You could spend weeks exploring North East Scotland. Don't be overly ambitious with what can be crammed into a couple of days. North East Scotland is charming when you take your time and absorb the inspiring impressions of Scotland that seems to come directly from your own imagination.

Accommodation in North East Scotland: There are excellent historic accommodations available in the region's range of historic towns, like Perth and St. Andrews. Like the region, the accommodation has a decidable Scottish feel, with huge fried breakfasts and great views.

The cathedral ruins at St. Andrews

North East Scotland Experiences

In a Few Days

This region is not be rushed and with a few days it's more enjoyable to soak up the atmosphere in an area that's closer to Edinburgh and the Central Belt. This is based on two historic towns, Perth and St. Andrews, with options to wind into the landscapes as a day excursion. The following are all within an easy couple of hours from the Central Belt and can be easily combined.

- Seaside **St. Andrews** is a treasure chest of panoramas and history. This is one of Scotland's finest destinations, situated on a stellar coastline and as highbrow as it's possible to get in Scotland. While a day trip can give you a taste of the architecture, a few days is recommended.

    o Aimlessly **wander through the town** and there's dozens of boutiques, cafes, bars, and buildings that revel in their medieval pomp. It's an ideal afternoon introduction to the town. The **St. Andrews Visitors Centre** has been refurbished and is a good source of information for what's on at the many theaters.

    o To understand more about the history and architecture of the town, try the **St. Andrews Preservation Trust Museum**.

    o **St. Andrews Cathedral** was the largest in Scotland and it retains its resplendence despite most of it lying in ruins. There's a real sense of history as you walk through the stone archways and take photos beneath centuries of masonry.

    o St. Andrews is widely regarded as being where the sport of golf was invented. The old **St. Andrews Golf Course** often hosts the Open Championship and is always in the top echelons of the world's most beautiful courses. You'll struggle to play here, but head to the 18th hole for a photo of the **Swilcan Burn Bridge** beneath the clubhouse, one of golf's most eternal pictures. To try and understand the sport, the **British Golf Museum** is far more interesting than it sounds.

- Prince William and his wife Kate studied at the **University of St. Andrews**, one of the most illustrious institutions in the whole of Britain. The famous couple are far from the first royals to study here. The grounds and library buildings befit this regal status and are definitely worth a look. Then head further inside to the free **Museum of the University of St. Andrews**, one that's stuffed with jewelry and art from through the ages. The **University of St. Andrews Observatory** is also well worth a look.

- Patrolling the headland due north of the town, the crumbling remains of **St. Andrews Castle** provide a great focal point for photos of the coastline.

- The **St. Andrews beaches** aren't those for sunbathing and swimming, but the cliffs and sand offer some easy hiking trails with wonderful vistas.

- Only a short drive out of town, **Craigtoun Country Park** is one for the whole family; ice creams, forest walking trails, tea shops...you can picture what it's like right?

- A good half day trip from St. Andrews is to head south. **Scotland's Secret Bunker** is a weird ode to war and old-school electronic systems, then the villages of **Kingsbarns** and **Crail** are places of whitewashed houses and sipping an ale.

- Both brewery and distillery, **Eden Mill** is rapidly developing its reputation and is a great choice for anyone who knows absolutely nothing about whisky or ale. Extremely knowledgable guides ensure you're not embarrassed to ask obvious questions.

• Containing some of Scotland's finest buildings, Perth offers a complete submersion in the heritage of the country, including castles, churches, whisky, gardens, and pubs. It's a strong rival to St. Andrews for a visitor's attention. Perth is perhaps more atmospheric but St. Andrews has the more elegant backdrop.

- The last King of Scotland (the actual king, not the guy from the movie) was coronated at **Scone Palace**, a historic house that can rival any other in Britain. Come for tea and scones with a view over the inspiring grounds, and then explore the lavishly decorated interiors.

- **Balhousie Castle** isn't as visually impressive but has a great museum (**The Black Watch Castle and Museum**) that charts Britain's involvement in war over the last few centuries.

- Another two castle (yes, there's a lot in Perth) are **Elcho Castle**, a 16th century tower of stone and turrets for cannons. Built around a moat and imposing in its faded glory, Elcho also has great grounds. **Huntingtower Castle** is smaller but similar, this time the towers dating to lordly residence in the 15th century.

Huntingtower Castle near Perth

- A relic of the 18th century industrial revolution, **Historic Scotland Stanley Mills** is a huge complex of old brick warehouses and preserved industrial equipment. Both poignant and thought provoking, it helps to recreate a rich and then poor time in Perth's history.

- Two churches continue the look at Perth's original architecture. The **Kirk of St. John the Baptist** and **St. Serf's Church** are peaceful shelters whenever the rain comes down.

- Drinkers will be fond of Perth. **The Inveralmond Brewery** is a chance to sample ales and all the local pubs seem to have something local on the hand pull. **Strathearn Distillery** provides something with a much higher alcohol content.

- When traveling between the Central Belt and the towns of Perth and St. Andrews you can get a strong sense of the region's natural beauty.

  - **Loch Leven Castle** has great views over the loch itself and a **heritage walking trail** skirts the edge of the tranquil water.

  - **Lomond Mills Regional Park** is an excellent spot for a picnic and easy walk. On its eastern boundary, the **Falkland Palace and Gardens** shimmer on a sunny day but can be a little moribund in winter.

  - Dunfermline is certainly worth visiting for two excellent attractions. The **Dunfermline Abbey and Palace** combines two of Scotland's travel paradigms: regal splendor and evocative ruin. **Carnegie Hall** and the **Andrew Carnegie Birthplace Museum** are odes to the educational pioneer who had a huge influence on university education around the world, particularly in the USA.

  - Further east along the coast towards St. Andrews, **Aberdour Castle** and **Inchcolm Abbey** have mesmerizing locations along the coast. **Kirkcaldy** is the next village along and the beaches start to impress from here. A succession of villages then mark the journey towards St. Andrews, all of them worthy of a lunch stop if you have your own transport.

- To the west of Perth and easily connected with Stirlingshire (see chapter 7), the village of **Crieff** is home to the **Famous Grouse Experience**, a journey through one of the country's most famous distilleries. Note famous, not necessarily best. If driving from Glasgow to Perth this is the place to break the journey.

In a Week or More

With more time you can really explore the region, heading north to a gorgeous landscape dotted with ruins, beaches, castles, and retreats. Further north, the journeys can begin to take up a large chunk of your time, especially if you don't have your own transport. Be patient, because the bus always comes, it just takes a while to get there. After checking out some of the experiences in a few days or more (above), these help continue your journey north through Scotland.

- **Dundee** could also be considered a potential base for those with only a few days on the North East Coast. While not as picturesque as Perth or St. Andrews, the coastal city has an eclectic bunch of attractions and a lively local atmosphere.

    o **Discovery Point** is the city's main tourist attraction, a large royal ship which charts maritime and regal chronicles in Scotland. **HM Frigate Unicorn** is a more alluring ship but has been closed for the last year.

    o The city's architecture is a mishmash of styles but the remaining old buildings are also nice places to spend a morning, or afternoon. These include the **Mills Observatory**, **Camperdown Country Park**, **Broughty Castle**, and the **McManus**. The latter is certainly the grandest and doubles as the city museum.

    o Laying claim to Scotland's dedication to quirky art and industry, Dundee's galleries are likely to be loved by some but not all. **Verdant Works** is colorful and filled with clanging metal, while **Dundee Conteporary Arts** has a confusing mix of exhibits.

- Just north of Dundee is **Forfar**. Imposingly situated on its outskirts is **Glamis Castle**, set in wide grounds of vivacious green. Nearby **Kirriemuir** is also worth a stop for lunch or a drink.

- Taking the coastal road from Dundee, you pass through **Carnoustie** and its seaside fisherman splendor, then **Arbroath**, a historic town that's only recently understanding its potential as a tourism destination. **St Vigeans Sculptured Stones** and the **Arbroath Abbey** can both be visited in a couple of hours.

- Along the coast, the next obvious place to linger is **Montrose**, a cute village that's within easy reach of some smaller and even cuter villages. By this point the beaches and bays become real delights, the sand usually empty and the cliffs providing an iconic backdrop. In particular, see **Lunan Bay** just south of Montrose. Nearby **Brechin** has a small and elegant cathedral, while **Edzell Castle** is as enchanting as the village of **Edzell** itself.

- **Coastal Aberdeen** is one of Scotland's most loved cities; small enough to feel local but big enough to compel for a few days. North of the city you'll find **long sandy beaches**, complete with beach bars and surfers returning shivering from the North Sea. **Balmedie** is the most popular. 17Th century **Craigievar Castle** and **St. Machar's Cathedral** are the city's architectural highlights, however, Aberdeen isn't a necessarily a place of ticking off the sights. It's one for soaking up the ambiance.

- Nestled at the entrance to the **Cairngorms** (see below), **Pitochry** is both a starting point for adventures in the mountains and a chance to really see village life. It's unmissable attraction is **Edradour Distillery**, one of the finest in Scotland, and within stumbling distance of the Pitcohry hotels.

- As you head into the mountains you pass by some precipitous peaks which make for challenging day hikes, like **Ben Vrackie**. Continuing on the A9 you reach **Blair Castle**, much like other Scottish castles but with a staggering mountain backdrop.

- The far north of this region is a rural juxtaposition of quaint villages, unspoiled beaches, and rural retreats. There's less in the way of core attractions, and more in the way of cottages to disappear into and spend a week recharging the batteries. **Balmedia, Buchan,** and **Cullen**, all have splendid beaches, but there's little to choose between any of the sandy stretches that enclose the area. Public transport in this area is a challenge. But with a car, this ia a place for randomly driving down country trails and admiring how untouched and unchanged the region feels.

- Coated in snow for much of the winter and imperiously high at all times, the **Cairngorms National Park** is the geological barrier between the Highlands (see chapter 10) and North East Scotland. It's the country's **premier ski destination** and a site of some fine single and multi day hiking trails. A series of lochs provide the next piece of the renowned Scotland landscape, **Loch Muich** being a good option if you're with public transport. This is a very rural and remote place, with most villages featuring little more than a pub and a seemingly abandoned church. **Linn O' Dee** is a lovely area that gives a showcase of highlands scenery within each reach of Aberdeen. Note that the western side of Cairngorms is featured in the next chapter.

Skiing in Cairngorms National Park

Chapter 10:
The Scottish Highlands and Islands

Rugged and near deserted, the Scottish Highlands are one of Europe's great stretches of wilderness. It's a place of almost unrivaled natural splendor, the mountains cascading towards white sand beaches and scenes that wouldn't be out of place on a tropical island. Lochs offer an iconic focal point, big and small expanses of water dominating most vistas. Starting at Loch Lomond National Park (see chapter 7) the Highlands run up the western half of the country to the northern tip at John 'o' Groats. The boundaries of the area are clearly marked by geography, separating the Highlands from the lowlands (all the areas in chapters 5 to 9).

The peace, the serenity, the vast expanses of national park...the Scottish Highlands is a destination that requires exploration and a sense of adventure. Other than a couple of towns, the urban centers are rarely bigger than one street villages, while the winding roads are not for quick and easy travel. Yet those who can devote time to the region will invariably say it's their highlight of Scotland, if not the whole of Europe. Just beware that the Highlands can get very cold and icy, not just in winter. You'll need a few thick layers and a good rain coat regardless of the season.

Sharing a Gaelic culture with the Highlands, Scotland has three groups of islands, each battered by the weather and pertaining the most traditional examples of traditional life. Most are extraordinarily remote and bewilderingly impressive. Take a tent, bring your raincoat, and it's easy to imagine that you're half way to the Arctic. While destinations in their own right, they're included here as you must travel through the Highlands to reach the islands. Unless you've got a week to spare, the islands form a part of a Highland's itinerary.

- Running off the western Scottish coast, the **Hebrides** are most accessible for those wanting a day or two exploring an island.

- Just off the far north coast, the World Heritage **Orkney Islands** have been inhabited for 8000 years and the Scots will joke that little has changed since neolithic times.

- Halfway to Northern Scandinavia, the **Shetland Islands** are breathtakingly remote and bizarre.

Loch Lomand

Travel Essentials for the Scottish Highlands

Getting Here: The small Inverness Airport offers an alternative entry point to traveling from Glasgow or Edinburgh. Flights land here from a variety of British and European cities. Regular trains also connect London / Edinburgh / Glasgow to Inverness. The West Highland Railway runs a service from Glasgow to some towns on the western coast of Scotland. Otherwise, it's a slow bus or drive heading through the mountains.

Getting Around: Bus services in the Scottish Highlands are surprisingly good and they always come with astonishing vistas. Much of the Highlands experience is about the views, and they're no different by bus or private car. However, the buses are sporadic and forward planning is essential. Furthermore, they're not as effective in connecting the smallest villages and national parks. The best option for really exploring is to hire a car, either from Glasgow or Inverness.

Itinerary Planning: The Highlands requires and deserves time. While a couple of destinations can be reached on a two to three day excursion from the cities, the region's remoteness and wild beauty takes more than a few days.

Where to Stay: Accommodation here is as Scottish as it comes. Expect spacious rooms, incredible views from the window, and villages that are eerily quiet once the pub closes at 11pm.

Scottish Highlands Experiences

Less than One Week

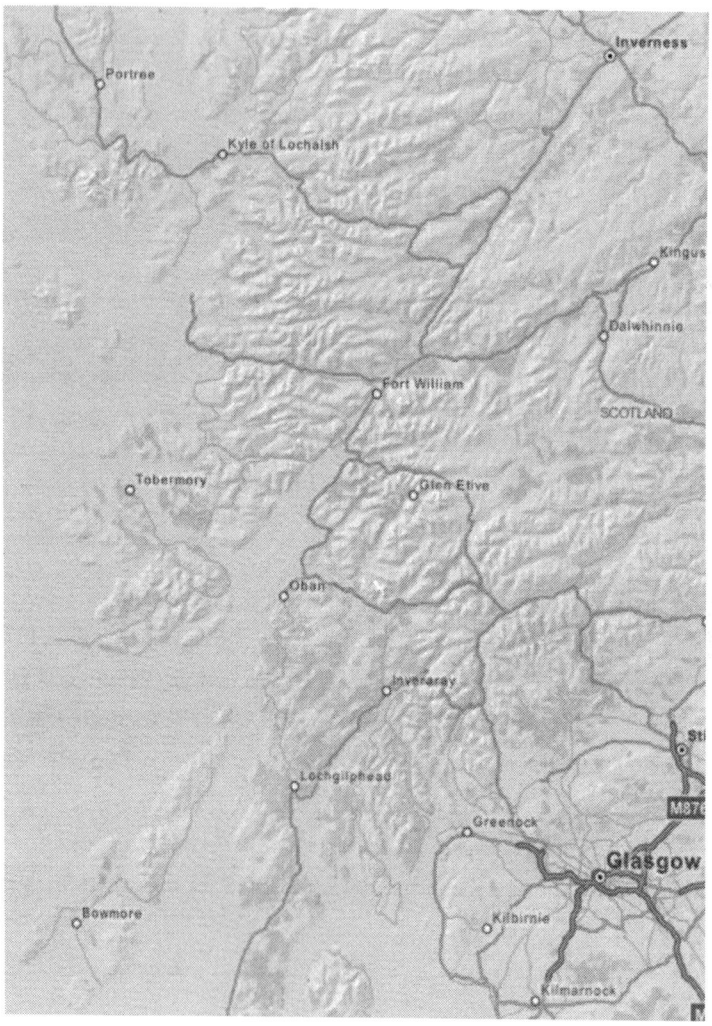

To get the most from the Highlands in a short amount of time, there are two options. Base yourself in one of the destinations that are easiest to reach: Loch Lomand, Fort William, Oban, or Inverness. Or take a journey north through these destinations to Inverness, where there's easy transport back to the Central Belt. All the following are listed from south to north.

- **Loch Lomand & The Trossachs National Park** marks the start of the Scottish Highlands. It's covered in chapter 7 – The Central Belt – because it offers the easiest day trip and glimpse at the region's beauty. A succession of lochs and hiking trails provide the highlights. Continue through the park, ascending and then descending, ascending and descending again, to reach **Inveraray**, where **Inverary Jail** and **Inverary Castle** command beautiful locations beneath the park's peaks.

Inveraray Castle

- There are few roads through the mountains so most journeys will follow the same route. From Inverary the road skirts a narrow loch to **Kilchurn Castle**, another old fortress made more impressive by the backdrop.

- Windswept **Oban** offers adventure on the coast. It's scattered with medieval relics, like the walls of **McCaig's Tower** and moss covered remains of **Dunollie**, a castle crumbling into the water. The town is quaint enough but most people come to get wet, either via **kayaking tours** or rock climbing above icy waters at **Stramash**. **Ganavan Sands** beach is a glimpse at the endless untrammeled sand as you head further into the Highlands. Just north of the town, on **Loch Linnhe,** the **Scottish Sea Life Sanctuary** is good for seals and other blubbery marine mammals.

- Oban is the terminal for ferries to a number of the **Hebrides Islands**. The **Isle of Mull** is less than 30 minutes away and an excellent day trip option. Dock besides **Duart Castle** then take local buses across the wilderness to some of the most spectacular coastal scenery in the country. Much further afield, **South Uist** and **North Uist** are iconically remote and a place for taking the tent and hiking boots.

- **Glencoe** combines the three classic ingredients of Highland travel. It's situated on a loch, with views gazing across the water onto fields of sheep and dry stone walls. Behind the village are towering mountains and a mix of hiking trails for all fitness levels (in particular check out **Glencoe Mountain**). And finally, there's plenty of local atmosphere to keep you entertained: yes, people still where kilts here.

- Sandwiched between the northern tip of Loch Linnhe and Ben Nevis (see below), **Fort William** is perhaps the Highlands' most beautiful and accessible town. It's surrounded by nature reserves and the emphasis is on **outdoor adventure**. The following are all one or even overnight tours: **Steall Waterfall**, **canoeing on the loch**, hiking in **Creag Meagaidh National Nature Reserve**, and walking the hills of **Glen Roy**. Interludes from the outdoors are offered by history, not as impressive as elsewhere but nevertheless with a certain charm: **Inverlochy Castle** and the **West Highland Museum** are the most popular.

- Scotland and Britain's highest peak is **Ben Nevis**, a craggy mountain that stands just east of Fort William. It's a full day hike to get up and down the mountain on foot, although the achievement is slightly spoiled when you discover there's also a **sky gondola** to the summit. On a clear day, the views are astonishing, although there's a very strong chance that you'll be standing in a cloud of mist. If taking the gondola, there are a succession of short (less than one hour) **hiking loops** signposted at the summit, and for half the year you'll be in the snow.

- Running between Fort William and Inverness, skirting Loch Ness, the **West Highland Way** is one of Scotland's most dramatic. The same route by **rural railway** is equally impressive.

- Most people have heard of the **Loch Ness Monster**. Unfortunately, nobody has ever seen it. Still, tens of thousands of tourists – predominantly American and Asian – descend on **Fort Augustus** and **Drumnadrochit** in search of the fictional swamp dinosaur. Both towns specialize in **boat trips on Loch Ness**, along with Nessy art galleries and tacky souvenirs. As beautiful as Loch Ness is, there are less famous, less crowded, and less expensive options nearby (e.g. Glencoe).

- **Cairngorms National Park** divides the Highlands from the Scottish Lowlands and the South East of the country (eastern parts of this park are covered in chapter 9). The Western half of Scotland's largest national park is the more famous, dominated by a series of staggering peaks, most notably, **Cairngorm Mountain**. Around the villages of **Kingussie** and **Aviemore**, you'll find Scotland's finest hiking trails, taking you through **Glenmore Forest Park** to peaks and **hidden crater lochs**. This area also has a **winter ski season**.

- Britain's northernmost city, and the capital of the Highlands, **Inverness** is somewhat of a halfway house between rural exploration and city sights. Thanks to its excellent transport connects it's also regarded as the **Gateway to the Highlands**; you'll find dozens of tour companies operating single and multi day trips further afield if you're traveling independently. While it is a gateway, Inverness doesn't have the astonishing surrounding vistas of towns in the nearby area.

    o Dissecting the town, **River Ness** makes for a beautiful short walk and immersion in the calmness of Inverness. Many riverside cafes and pubs could see you losing a day. Just uphill from the water, the **Inverness Museum and Art Gallery** is a good rainy day option.

    o A 30 minute bus ride north, **Nairn** has one of Britain's finest beaches, a huge blindingly white expanse of sand surrounded with cliffy hiking trails.

    o Scotland isn't short of battlefields and stories of bloodshed, **Culloden Battlefield** is one of the best and bloodiest: take a guide.

    o The vast **Highlanders' Museum** has a regal focus, containing the region's history and some of the queen's art collection.

    o **St. Andrews Cathedral** dominates the burgeoning city, although it's not got the pomp of those in Scotland's other cities.

    o For the most part, Inverness is a central point for **getting out and exploring** any of the Highland areas in this chapter.

With a Week or More

Journey slowly and plan inconsistently. This region is best when you succumb to the nature and soak up the tranquility. With more time, the destinations listed above can be really savored, with plenty of days set aside for hiking trails and nature exploration. Alternatively, journey up to Inverness and then keep going, exploring these experiences in the far north of the Highlands.

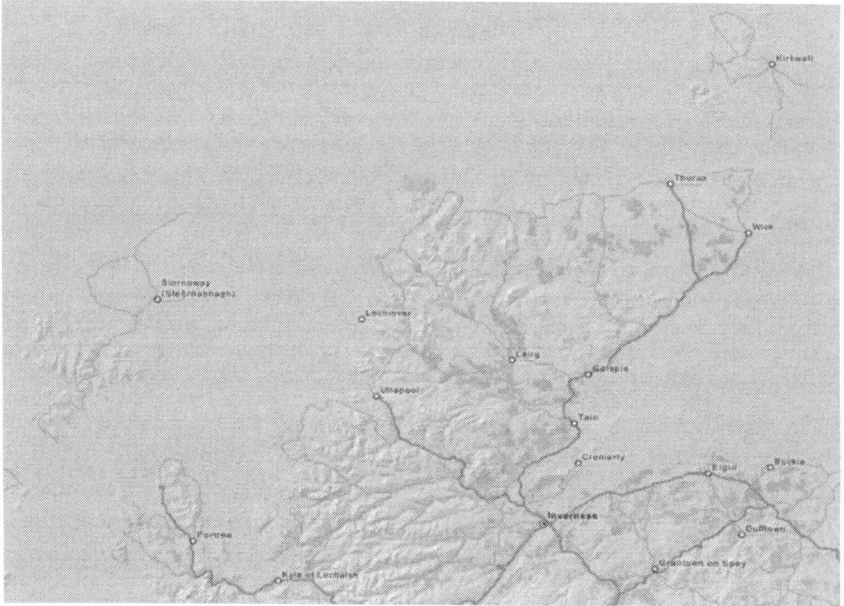

- Heading west of Inverness, the wonderful **Kyle Line railway** is one of Britain's most scenic. Choose to get off at **Loch Carron,** or continue to **Kyle of Lochalsh** and eat some fish and chips while looking across the water to the Isle of Skye.

- The most accessible and largest of the Hebrides, the **Isle of Skye** is connected to Kyle by bridge, making it ideal for a day trip if you have your own transport. Once on the island you'll want to stay longer though. Vast stretches of scarred valleys roll in every direction, compelling anyone to start walking. Due to better roads, most visitors head to Skye's northwestern tips: the **castle at Dunvegan**, the dazzling **Claigan Coral Beach**, mystical **Faerie Glen**, and the well marked hiking trails around **The Old Man of Stoor.**

- Skye's greatest attraction is the **Quaraing**, a series of huge massive land slips that tumble from from cliffs to the ocean. Bizarre and photogenic, the landscapes come from the annals of the world's weirdest and most wonderful.

- There are essentially two routes through the northern half of the Highlands. Most spectacular but requiring your own wheels, a series of shockingly narrow roads run along the western shore, often skirting inland to circumnavigate a loch. The following run south to north from Kyle.

    - The journey is the chief attraction, the road continually fringed by green mountains, roaming sheep, and mist engulfed lochs. **Loch Ewe** is actually a fjord, coated in fog and spilling onto the Atlantic Ocean waves. **Loch Maree** is the biggest but you also skirt a few tiny lochs that resemble filming locations for a Scottish whisky commercial.

    - Ullapool appears on the roadsigns, but blink and you've already passed through it. Its **Visit Scotland Information Centre** is the best in the region.

    - Further north and it's rare you pass anything but sheep. This is a popular area for **hiring an old stone cottage** and escaping from the world for a week. On a sunny day **Achmelvich Beach** is more Indian Ocean than Northern Scotland. Adjacent **Clachtoll Beach** is equally white and pure.

    - Continue past dozens of lochs until you reach **Durness** on the northern coast. The wide and shimmering **Balnakeil Bay** is just one of many stunning beaches in the area. While it's rarely sunbathing weather, it's also rare to spot a set of footprints in the sand. From here, the road continues east to **Thurso** and joins the Highlands Eastern route (see below).

    - Between Kyle and Durness there are hundreds of bays, mountains and lochs, that could be listed here. If you're self-sufficient, this is a chance to getaway into one of the **last remaining wilderness areas of Europe**.

- Cut adrift in the Atlantic, the **Isle of Lewis** and **Isle of Harris** are reached via a ferry to **Stornoway** from Ullapool, Oban, and Isle of Skye. Both these islands submerge you in **Gaelic culture** and are best when you have a few days to spare.

- An eastern route up the Highland's pinnacle isn't as remote, although each of the villages you pass are remarkably small. While not quite as dramatic, this route is achievable with public transport. The following are listed south to north.

    - The most spectacular section of scenery starts after you cross **Dornoch Firth**. Regularly in lists of Britain's top beaches, **Dornoch Beach** is surrounded by vivacious greenery that shines despite the clouds. With its **quaint pubs and historic cathedral**, **Dornoch** makes a good place to spend the night.

    - **Golspie** and **Brora** seaside villages send whiffs of fish and chips through the fisher houses. **Brora's beach** is outstanding while **Dunrobin Castle** commands a remote cliffside perch near Golspie.

    - The next obvious overnight stop is **Wick**, home to **Pulteney Distillery** and the inevitable drunken evening. Within walking distance of town are more **excellent beaches**.

    - Keep heading north and the road swings around **John o' Groats**, Britain's most northerly mainland point and an iconic photo stop. There's not much here other than a lighthouse and hazy sea view, but it's worth the detour for a photo with the sign.

    - The largest town in this area is **Thurso**, 30 minutes southwest of John o' Groats. Its sublime location and range of facilities make it an inevitable stop for anyone continuing this far north in Scotland. Thurso is also the port for ferries to the Orkney and Shetland Islands.

- To cross from the east to west coastlines, the easiest route is via **Lairg**, a cute little village on **Loch Shin**. Endless hiking trails can be found around here, particularly at **Alladale Wilderness Reserve**. **Ravens Rock Gorge** and the **Falls of Shin** are the village's well advertised attractions, but just walking down the main road is an immersion in Highland nature. From Lairg, one road heads to the western beaches while another winds narrowly north to **Tonge, Loch Eriboll** and **Durness.**

- Jutting into the ocean, just off the northern coast, the **Orkney Islands** are accessible as a day trip from Thurso. A scattering of **Neolithic remains** hint at the islands' history while a **continually rolling landscape** is a surreal place to explore on foot. **Mainland** is the largest island. If you have more time, especially in summer, a short ferry sailing take you to **virtually uninhabited islands** for settling in and escaping the world.

- Much further north (over 100miles from the mainland), the **Shetland Islands** offer a glimpse at Arctic landscapes but you'll need to devote a few days. **Unspoiled scenery and snow lined cliffs** make for dazzling days of exploration. Scalloway and Lerwick are the only towns, both make good bases. **Mainland** is the largest island and the easiest to access; like the others, it's a treasure trove of lochs, precipitous valleys, and women dressed in locally knitted tartan. Out of over 100, **only a dozen islands are inhabited**, so if you have a tent and your own food, this could be an absolute escape. But it's cold and foggy almost all year round, with vast fields of show dominating the winter.

Chapter 12:
Thanks for Reading!

After reaching the end of Scotland you can hear the bagpipes in the distance and feel the single malt on the back of the throat. You're wearing a souvenir kilt and checking photos to see if the gray lump is a rock or the Loch Ness Monster. Hopefully this travel guide is also still with you as your adventure in Scotland comes to an end. And if you haven't set foot in the country just yet, then all these iconic moments are set to come.

So thank you for reading. If you hadn't been reading then there would have been no point writing. The aim of this guide is to open up Scotland to the independent traveler, providing the signposts that open up one of the world's most underrated and sublime countries. We'd love to hear from you, regardless of whether this guide was a trusty bible or discarded like a 13th century Scottish castle covered in moss. We continue to built our network of guides because of all the positive feedback, so if this one didn't hit the mark then get in touch. We're eager to improve.

So, thank you once again. And if you want to really thank us, the author is probably propped on a bar stool in one of Scotland's whisky distilleries. Don't buy him another drink. It would be thanks enough to show him the way home...

Enjoy your trip!

Dagny Taggart

Learn Any Language 300% FASTER

>> Get Full Online Language Courses With Audio Lessons <<

Would you like to learn a new language before you start your trip? I think that's a great idea. Now, why don't you do it 300% *FASTER*?

I've partnered with the most revolutionary language teachers to bring you the very language online courses I've ever seen. It's a mind-blowing program specifically created for language hackers such as ourselves. It will allow you learn ANY language, from French to Chinese, 3x faster, straight from the comfort of your own home, office, or wherever you may be. It's like having an unfair advantage!

You can choose from a wide variety of languages, such as French, Spanish, Italian, German, Chinese, Portuguese, and A TON more.

Each Online Course consists of:

+ 91 Built-In Lessons
+ 33 Interactive Audio Lessons
+ 24/7 Support to Keep You Going

The program is extremely engaging, fun, and easy-going. You won't even notice you are learning a complex foreign language from scratch. And before you realize it, by the time you go through all the lessons you will officially become a truly solid speaker.

Old classrooms are a thing of the past. It's time for a revolution.

If you'd like to go the extra mile, follow the link below, and let the revolution begin!

>> http://bitly.com/foreign-language-courses <<

CHECK OUT THE COURSE »

PS: Can I Ask You a Quick Favor?

If you liked the book please leave a nice review on Amazon! I'd absolutely love to hear your feedback. Please go to Amazon right now (following the link below), and write down a quick line sharing with me your experience. I personally read ALL the reviews there, and I'm thrilled to hear your feedback and honest motivation. It's what keeps me going, and helps me improve everyday =)

Go to Amazon and drop me a quick review! Thank you!

***

**ONCE YOU'RE BACK,
FLIP THE PAGE!
BONUS CHAPTER AHEAD
=)**

Preview Of "Italy For Tourists - The Traveler's Travel Guide to Make the Most Out of Your Trip to Italy - Where to Go, Eat, Sleep & Party"

Introduction
Are You Ready for an Amazing Journey?

Italy is undoubtedly one of the most sought after travel destinations worldwide. From its sweeping landscapes and old world feel to the hustling and bustling metropolises, lazy farm towns, countryside vineyards, historic architecture and culture, and of course, delectably delicious cuisine, there's no wonder why Italy tops the list of places to visit for the seasoned world traveler and first time travelers alike looking to experience their very own "la dolce vita" ...the good life to those who don't speak Italian.

Italy definitely doesn't disappoint with the seemingly endless travel destinations it has to offer. The eclectic landscapes alone are enough to draw outdoor enthusiasts from across the globe. In fact, Italy is home to the most UNESCO World Heritage sites out of all the countries in the world! If that's not impressive enough to the seasoned traveler, there's always the wide array of landscapes sure to please even the hardest to impress tourist. Where else can you find vineyards or volcanoes, mountains or beautiful beaches, historic ruins or modern cities? The answer lies in all that Italy has to offer upon your arrival.

Aside from the endless supply of breathtaking landscapes, Italy also has much to offer in the way of historical cities as well. From Rome to Florence and from Venice to Naples, there's plenty to see when it comes to Ancient Roman Empire architecture, towering glorious cathedrals, as well as such as vast array of history, culture, and art. Italy offers those seeking out splendid palaces of former kings and queens a chance to revel in ancient times, while giving those interested in the magnificent wonders of art and architecture brought on by the Renaissance a chance to marvel at the sheer talent and awe of it all.

When speaking in terms of Italy, it's inevitable that one's mind will most likely think food. Italian cuisine, however, can be as diverse as the regions it comes from. For instance, in the north, you may tend to run into French and Austrian influences when you dine, meaning you may find things tend to be rich in butter, cream, rice, and meat. Heading into the central and southern regions, the cooking tends to get lighter, with use of olive oils, tomatoes, eggplants, and fish. And of course, what's a trip to Italy without pizza and pasta? For those who love wine and cheese, visiting Italy can prove to be a true gastronomical delight, with different regions boasting their own specialty cheeses, sausages, or salami. And with so many types of wine and the famous sparkling Italian Prosecco, there will be much food and drink to revel in when it comes to your Italian getaway.

So now that you've decided to plan a trip to Italy, the main question may be: Where do you begin? Do you take in the scenic beauty of the Alps and embark on a romantic gondola ride along the famous canals of Venice after spending a whirlwind day in the busting, modern city of Milan all while taking in all that Northern Italy has to offer? Do you opt for venturing through the historic streets of Rome and seeing the great architectural feats of the Ancient Romans or perhaps venturing into the quieter, more laid back Umbria Region where the slow pace doesn't take away from the equally historic sites and feel of an old world Italy, all of this while traveling through Italy's Central Region. Or perhaps you'd like to indulge in the pristine beauty of the Amalfi Coast, take in the art, culture, and pizza in majestic Naples, and see the amazing history of Pompeii while opting for Italy's Southern Region. And just when you think you've got way too many Italy travel destinations to choose from, don't forget about the fabulous islands of Italy. Whether you want to bask in the glamour of Capri, take in the old world culture and cuisine of Sicily while getting a view of Mt. Etna, or visit the eclectic, yet historic Sardinia, there's definitely plenty of excellent choices for those wanting an Italian island experience.

In this comprehensive guide, you'll be introduced to the various regions of Italy, popular cities, and tourist destinations to go to, as well as some "off the beaten path" spots if you're looking for a more laid back, less touristy trip. You'll get up to date information on where to stay, eat, and the best way to get around, as well as find helpful tips on how to make the most out of your Italian travel experience. So now it's time to sit back in your gondola, sip your Italian wine, and enjoy planning your amazing trip to Italy!

Italy Overview
The Most Beautiful Italian Regions

Due to its vast land size, Italy can be divided up into three general regions. From there they are then divided up into more specific regions similar to states like in the US. Then there are also the islands of Italy to cover as well. The country of Italy itself is divided into the Northern, Central, and Southern Regions, with each one having its own sense of culture, history, cuisine, and dialect. Where you chose to visit in Italy depends on a number of factors. There are many questions you can ask yourself including: What cities are on my list of places to see in Italy? Do I want to go to the beach? Do I want to go wine tasting at various vineyards? What museums do I wish to visit? The questions can truly be endless, but the answers can be summed up into the three general regions of Italy, or with the various island options. In the following chapters, each general region and the islands will be broken down into places to see and visit, making it easier to plan your Italian destination getaway.

Within each general regional section of Italy, we will explore more specific regions and the cities within them that are great to visit. The guide also includes some great Italian islands to explore as well. There will also be places to visit listed geared toward those who are looking for a more nature involved vacation such as going to a national park or lake. And of course, for those looking to immerse themselves in the vast cultural Italian heritage and history, we'll take a look at museums and popular historical places to see. You'll also find tips on places to stay as well as where to indulge in some heavenly Italian cuisine. So, without further delay, let's dive into the North, Central, South, and Islands of Italy!

CHAPTER 1
Northern Italy (Valle d'Aosta, Liguria, Veneto & More)

Overview

The Northern region of Italy boasts some spectacular landscapes. Not only that, but it's here in the Northern region where you'll find Milan, the fashion capital of the world, and Venice, where you can explore history in one of the world's most romantic settings. On top of all of the historic cities to see, there's also the amazing Alps, as well as the majestic, picturesque water vistas along the coasts.

- ✓ **Travel Tip:** When heading for Northern Italy, bypass the busy Rome International Airport and instead fly directly into Venice or Milan. This will save you time, especially if you plan to extensively explore the North. Adequate transportation from the airport is available to suit your needs as well.

Northern Italy tends to be a bit pricier than the rest of the country and boasts more updated technology than say, some of the more common farm villages to the south. Be sure to plan accordingly as far as expenses go so you're able to enjoy your trip to its fullest. Summers tend to be the busiest time here and the weather can get very hot. If you're looking for a more subdued getaway, fall and spring see much fewer tourists, and the weather is cooler. Unless you're planning on going to a ski resort, winter is not typically an ideal time to visit. Aside from the cold weather and snow, cities such as Venice also experience flooding in the winter.

Your options really are unlimited when you consider making Northern Italy party of your Italian itinerary. From the luxurious lakeside getaways, to the eclectic cities, to the towering cliff-lined seacoast, there's plenty to do and see while in this region. Who says you have to check out Renaissance paintings or set foot in an ancient cathedral? The beauty of your trip is that there are no rules when it comes to Italy, especially the Northern Region. So let's kick back, relax, and explore this section of Italy.

Milan

Overview:

For a taste of Italian culture without the typical feel of being in Italy, the face-paced metropolis of Milan is known for its fashion, thriving business, shopping, and nightlife. Where Rome tends to represent more of the old Italy feel, Milan shines as a newer, more modern Italian city. But don't worry, those looking to seek out the "old" Italy will still be able to find churches and architecture to suit your ancient history tastes. However, many say that Milan doesn't feel much like being in Italy at all. With its hustling and bustling way of life, this fashion and business capital keeps the locals busy. And with much of the architecture having the influence of an Austrian/German neoclassical look, you won't tend to find the more traditional Italian look of red terracotta roofs. Here limestone and other dark stone tend to be used for building. Make no mistake though, Milan has a style all its own and will provide lots to do and see while you visit there.

When to Visit:

Milan is a great place to visit all year round, but it's important to plan your trip according to the season the best suits you. Winters in Milan are often cold and can sometimes drop below zero degrees Celsius (32 degrees Fahrenheit). If winter is your thing though and you don't mind the foggy, rainy, and sometimes snowy weather, you may want to look into planning a holiday around Christmas time. The city becomes illuminated with a beautiful display of lights, and in front of the Duomo (the large gothic cathedral) a large Christmas tree is displayed. Of course, the one downside to visiting any large city during the holidays is the large crowds and busy streets due to all of the holiday shopping.

Spring and autumn tend to be the most ideal times to visit if you're looking for a quieter type of vacation. During these seasons, the locals are in work mode, leaving the streets mostly to the tourists. Autumns in Milan can be pretty rainy and foggy, while in the spring it can be quite pleasant. Spring is a good time to walk along a park and notice the trees blossoming. In the spring, Carnival time is a unique time to visit, as people dress up in costume and celebrate, as well as Easter time if you'd like to experience the services and celebrations held.

Summers in Milan tend to be very hot and humid. Most locals take their summer holidays in the month of August, so you may find certain shops and businesses closed during this month. If you're looking to have the city all to yourself, August would be the perfect time to visit, especially for those who hate crowds and too many tourists.

✓ **Travel Tip:** There are two international airports that service Milan: Malpensa (MXP) and Linate (LIN) Linate is a much smaller airport than the busy Malpensa, but it's very close to the center of the city. Malpensa has two runways and also two terminals. Both airports provide adequate transportation services as well.

What to See:

Milan offers an impressive variety of sights to see and things to do. From impressive museums and world class opera and theater houses to old churches and palaces, you're sure to find something that suits your travelling tastes. The lovely street and impressive squares combined with old architectural gems mixed in with the modern, striking buildings makes for a unique Milan experience. You'll also have the pleasure of seeing the oldest churches in all of Italy. Since Milan was the capital of the Northern Roman Empire, it boasts the most ancient churches of any other city across Europe!

The Duomo:

Yes, there are many churches and cathedrals to see in Milan, but the main one, especially for church enthusiasts, is The Duomo. This stunning cathedral is the main one of Milan and is located in Duomo Square. The massive, white marble constructed building was started in 1385, but construction lasted literally for centuries, finally being estimated finished around 1813. There are an impressive 3,159 statues in and around it, as well as beautiful altars and works of art to see inside. The Duomo is a definite must for those who appreciate stunning architecture and the history of churches in Italy.

Sforzesco Castle:

Long serving as a status symbol as well as a symbol of power for local and foreign rulers, the impressive Storzesco Castle, in its prime, once housed some of Milan's most influential leaders. It was saved from demolition in 1861 and renovated until 1905. The castle has four towers and has a courtyard where you'll see beautiful frescoes. Today it houses several museums called the Musei Civici which is spread out through several floors as well as throughout the Rocchetta and Ducal courtyard. There's an eclectic mix of artifacts from Ancient Egyptian to Italian, including an unfinished sculpture by Michelangelo. With its stunning, strong architecture and engaging museums, Sforzesco Castle is a must see for a glimpse of Milan's magnificent history.

Pinacoteca di Brera (Brera National Art Gallery):

Housed in the Palazzo di Brera, a palace built by Ancient Jesuits, the Pinacoteca di Brera is home to an impressive display of paintings by Italian masters dating from the fourteenth to the twentieth century. The building itself is also impressive, built in the Baroque style of architecture originally but then remodeled in the Neoclassical style later on. Inside, you'll find a science academy, an observatory, a library, and art academy, and the art gallery. In the gallery, art enthusiasts will be able to marvel at works by great such as Raphael, Caravaggio, Rubens, Jordaens, and Van Dyck.

Giardini Pubblici

Built between the years of 1782-1786 by the famed architect Giuseppe Piermarini, the Giardini Pubblici is a welcome park oasis in the middle of the concrete jungle that is Milan. It's a great place for a stroll when you want to take a break from the busy tourist spots in the actual city. Here you'll find trees, springs, a lake, and many beautiful statues. After your stroll, if you're up for more exploring, you can visit the Natural History Museum and Planetarium on the park's eastern edge along Corso Venezia.

Fashion District:

What's a trip to Milan without visiting the famous Fashion District? In a city known for being the capital of all things fashion, here you'll find some of the best shopping opportunities in all of Europe. It's here where you're likely to find many upscale choices like Versace, Armani, Bulgari, Chanel, and Dolce & Gabbana, just to name a few. For those who don't have a designer clothing budget, more affordable shopping options are offered as well. There's also some beautiful architecture to admire along the streets of the Fashion District, including majestic mansions from the seventeenth to nineteenth centuries. A few of these mansions also house museums for those who are tired of shopping and would like to take in a bit of culture.

- ✓ **Travel Tip:** If the idea of trying to figure out what all to see while you're staying in Milan seems a little too daunting, there are some great guided tour options, including walking tours that will give you exclusive access to da Vinci's "The Last Supper" painting without having to wait in the long line. Private and group walking tours are available that take you throughout the city and can be a great way to see the key attractions of Milan.

- ✓ **Travel Tip:** Keep in mind that most museums in Milan are closed on Mondays, so it's a good idea to plan your itinerary accordingly.

Where to Eat:

Milan is rich with delicious cuisine and the locals are pretty traditional when it comes to authentic Italian cooking. There are an abundance of restaurants, trattorias, and enoteche (wine bars) to cater to whatever delectable cuisine you may be craving. The city's tastes tend to lend towards more filling, heavy meals that will satisfy even the most famished traveler.
- ✓ **Travel Tip:** Dining times in Milan tend to be a bit earlier than say those in Florence or Rome. The typical time for lunch tends to be between the hours of 12:30PM to 2:30 PM, while dinner tends to be from 7:30PM until 9:30PM.

When it comes to dining out in Milan, a great rule of thumb to follow is to dine where the locals are dining. For those who regularly show up for Happy Hour at restaurants and bars in their own country, you'll be thrilled to know that Milan has recently established its own version of Happy Hour or Aperitivo. There are a wide variety of eating establishments to choose from, including traditional Italian eateries, cafes, cheese and wine tasting bars, and upscale restaurants. And although the claim of being the birthplace of pizza belongs to Naples in the south of Italy, Milan still boasts some tasty pizza places as well.

- ✓ **Travel Tip:** It's best to avoid eating at restaurants situated around The Duomo, as these tend to be over-priced tourist traps with low quality food. Instead, try asking a local for a recommendation and stick with the advice of dining where the locals eat.

Nightlife:

For those looking for a night out on the town, Milan offers some great choices when it comes to having a good time. Check out Como Avenue, which is close to Garibaldi Station. It's lined with bars a clubs that tend to cater more towards the younger crowd. For a more sophisticated time, there a plenty of small pubs, bars, and cafes that are open late for your nighttime enjoyment. If you're looking for a bit more culture, Milan is home to some beautiful opera houses and theaters for taking in a night of opera or a play.

Where to Stay:

There are plenty of choices that will meet any sort of budget when it comes to finding accommodations in Milan. If camping is your thing, there's the Citta di Milano, a campsite located on the outskirts of the city. It has a restaurant, bar, and shower facilities, perfect for those looking to spend little on where they're staying so they can spend more for their travels around Milan. Hostels are also available and are often times very affordable. The Piero Rotta Youth Hostel and Ostello Olinda are two hostels that offer cheap rates and the Ostello Olinda also includes free Wi-Fi.

Hotels:

Like any large metropolitan city, hotel choices can range from very cheap to very expensive as well as reasonable rates somewhere in between. Some trustworthy budget hotels in Milan include the Boston Hotel, Dover Hotel, Hotel De Albertis, and the Hotel Garda. In the mid-range price, check out Ariston Hotel, Admiral Hotel, Hotel Cristallo, and Hotel Casa Mia. If you're looking to immerse yourself in all the luxury Milan has to offer, then you can look into the many upscale hotels such as Hotel Ascot, Hotel Lloyd, Hotel Pierre Milano, and Hotel De la Ville.

More Helpful Travel Tips:

- ✓ Avoid areas around Loreto, Central Station, and Porto di Mare (Southern end of the yellow metro line) at night, as these can be unsafe once it gets dark.

- ✓ Avoid migrant vendors in the streets selling "luxury" items as these are mostly fakes or imitations of the more expensive counterparts found in the Fashion District.

- ✓ Be wary of stranger trying to approach you to buy something. It's best to ignore the street peddlers and just keep walking.

- ✓ Enjoy all of the sights, sounds, tastes, and history Milan has to offer!

Click Here to Check out the Rest of "*Italy For Tourists*" on Amazon

Check Out My Other Books

Are you ready to exceed your limits? Then pick a book from the one below and start learning yet another new language. I can't imagine anything more fun, fulfilling, and exciting!

If you'd like to see the entire list of language guides (there are a ton more!), go to:

>>http://www.amazon.com/Dagny-Taggart/e/B00K54K6CS/<<

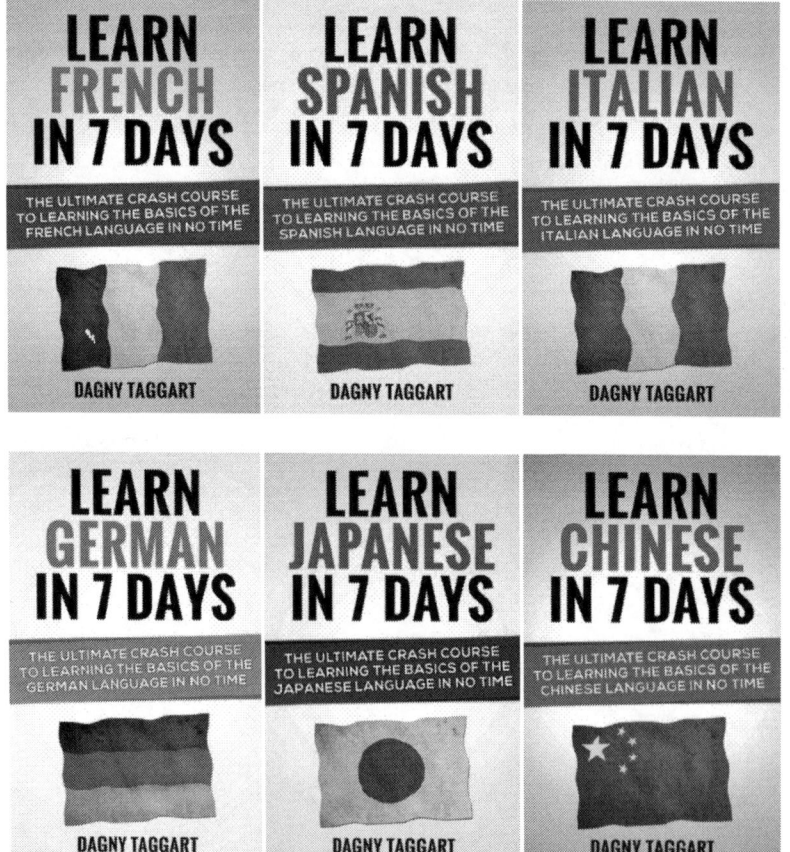

About the Author

Dagny Taggart is a language enthusiast and polyglot who travels the world, inevitably picking up more and more languages along the way.

Taggart's true passion became learning languages after she realized the incredible connections with people that it fostered. Now she just can't get enough of it. Although it's taken time, she has acquired vast knowledge on the best and fastest ways to learn languages. But the truth is, she is driven simply by her motive to build exceptional links and bonds with others.

She is inspired everyday by the individuals she meets across the globe. For her, there's simply not anything as rewarding as practicing languages with others because she gets to make friends with people from all that come from a variety of cultures. This, in turn, has broadened her mind and thinking more than she would have ever imagined it could.

Of course, as a result of her constant travels, Taggart has become an expert on planning trips and making the most of time spent out of what she calls her "base" town. She jokes that she's practically at the nomad status now, but she's more content to live that way.

She knows how to live on a manageable budget weather she's in Paris or Phnom Penh. She knows how to seek out the adventures and thrills, no doubt, lying in wait at any city she visits. She knows that reflection on each every experience is significant if she wants to grow as a traveler and student of the world's cultures.

Because of this, Taggart chooses to share her understanding of languages and travel so that others, too, can experience the same life-altering benefits she has.

Made in the USA
San Bernardino, CA
30 August 2015